OPPORTUNITIES IN
TRANSPORTATION

Adrian A. Paradis

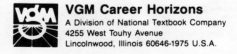

VGM Career Horizons
A Division of National Textbook Company
4255 West Touhy Avenue
Lincolnwood, Illinois 60646-1975 U.S.A.

TRANSPORTATION

Photo Credits

Front cover: Upper left, Santa Fe Railway
upper right, North American Van Lines; lower
left, Moran Towing; lower right, United Air
Lines. *Back cover:* Upper left, U.S. Army;
upper right, United Parcel Service; lower left,
United Air Lines; lower right, Washington
Metropolitan Area Transit Authority,
photographer Paul Myatt.

Copyright © 1983 by National Textbook Company
4255 West Touhy Avenue
Lincolnwood (Chicago), Illinois 60646-1975 U.S.A.
All rights reserved. No part of this book may
be reproduced, stored in a retrieval system, or
transmitted in any form or by any means, electronic,
mechanical, photocopying, recording or otherwise,
without the prior permission of National Textbook Company.
Manufactured in the United States of America.
Library of Congress Catalog Number: 82-62283

3 4 5 6 7 8 9 0 BB 9 8 7 6 5 4 3 2 1

ABOUT THE AUTHOR

Adrian A. Paradis was born in Brooklyn, New York, and graduated from Dartmouth College and Columbia University's School of Library Service. As a writer, businessman, vocational specialist, and researcher, he has published widely, with more than forty titles to his credit. He has covered subjects that range from banking to biographies, from public relations to religion, from vocational guidance to reference works, and from law to economics.

Mr. Paradis spent over twenty years as an officer of a major national corporation handling corporate matters, economic analysis, stockholder relations, corporate philanthropic contributions, security, and general administrative responsibilities. He and his wife Grace live in Canaan, New Hampshire, where he serves as editor of Phoenix Publishing, a small firm which specializes in regional trade books and New England town histories.

CONTENTS

The familiar train conductor's job provides opportunity for service as well as technical work. (Photo: Amtrak.)

CHAPTER 1

INTRODUCTION

Anne Potter, a young woman about 25 years old, leaned back in her chair and smiled at the elderly man sitting opposite her. Every inch of her small office was crowded. There were two desks, several straight chairs for customers, two filing cabinets, and a large bookcase crammed with timetables, books, and resort literature. Colorful travel posters covered the walls, and unusual cardboard plane models hung from the ceiling, twirling about slowly as the two people talked.

"I guess you might say I was born into a transportation family," Mrs. Potter said. "Two uncles were with the railroads, my father was with a larger trucker, and my mother was a former airline stewardess. So here I am, running a transportation agency, doing what I like best, which is working in the transportation field on a broad scale."

"Very interesting." The man stroked his chin thoughtfully. "I was a transportation man myself, until I retired. I was in long distance moving, and later in air freight." He paused briefly, smiled, and then asked, "Want to know why I brought my business here?" Mrs. Potter nodded. "The name on your window, 'Transportation Center,' intrigued me—the novelty of it and, I might say, the pretentiousness of calling such a small business in Chicago's Wabash Street a *Center*!"

The young woman laughed. "It all goes back to my college days," she said. "I was majoring in transportation, as was a classmate. You see," she continued, "my husband Frank and I had both been concentrating our studies on the business of moving people and things,

1

or to put it another way, the public conveyance of people and goods. And that's what we do now—we make every kind of arrangement for conveying people and goods in the air, over the land, or on the sea. What could be more complete?"

She paused briefly, then continued. "When Frank and I graduated, it was difficult deciding what we should do. Both of us loved to fly, and we enjoyed traveling by bus and train too. What's more, the movement of all kinds of goods—packages, household goods, and even freight—intrigued us. So first we did what was most important to us: we got married; and then, because we both liked all forms of transport, we decided to open this office so that we could become involved in everything to do with moving people and goods. We could have limited our business to being a travel agency or a shipping office, but we do it all—we arrange transport for almost anything. And we do it using nearly every form of transportation. Oh, excuse me."

She picked up the phone and a moment later hung up.

"Here's another example of how broad this business can be. That was a man who wants to ship his horse to California by air. It won't be too difficult. I know just the airline that's best equipped to handle animals, and we'll set it up for him." She looked down at the papers on the desk before her.

"Now, let's see about your reservations, Mr. Grant." She handed him an envelope. "Here are your tickets. When you get to San Francisco you'll have a choice of taking the bus or a cab into town. Or you can rent a car, and you'll find the rental desks to the left of the baggage claim area. By the way, there are plenty of places to park downtown. Transportation again: you can't get away from it! While we're on the subject, don't miss the bus trip which takes you around the city and out to the Golden Gate. I think you'll enjoy it."

"Thank you." Mr. Grant pushed the chair back and stood up. "I enjoyed meeting you and want to wish you and your husband lots of success. By the way, does he ever work here? I haven't seen him either time I've been in."

"Oh yes," she chuckled, "but right now Frank's away on a boat and plane trip to China. We have unique benefits in this business. This is a free trip to familiarize us with distant tourist spots. That's how I know about the buses and cabs in San Francisco. One of the airlines sponsored a visit to San Francisco and Hawaii recently." She nodded her head slightly. "Yes, Mr. Grant, this transportation business has it all over anything else, as far as Frank and I are concerned. In fact, I think you could say it's a way of life for us."

Obviously, for the young couple who own the "Transportation Center," the whole business of transporting people and goods is a satisfying way to experience a certain thrill and joy in living. Perhaps the same can be true for you if you choose a career in one of the many specialized areas of transportation.

Assume for a moment that you are a stewardess or steward on an airplane, one of several crew members taking care of a planeload of passengers. Your assignment calls for intensive training and a fine degree of cooperation with your fellow workers. In addition, you experience a spirit of camaraderie with your fellow employees as you work together and feed 100 or more passengers and perform the many other services which are part of the crew's responsibility. It is hard work and interesting, and usually there is a sense of accomplishment when you and your associates stand at the cabin door to say goodbye to the smiling and grateful passengers as they file off the plane.

Perhaps you are driving a huge tractor trailer loaded with lumber and pull in at a truck stop known for its good food. Here you meet other drivers and, over your coffee and doughnuts, exchange stories and renew friendships. It is almost a fringe benefit and provides an added plus to your job.

As a cab driver you can be your own boss, free to roam the city streets in search of fares. Each day brings new customers and new experiences, too, adding a certain zest to your life.

The same can be true if you are a seaman standing watch, while your huge vessel cuts through the rolling waves as the spray washes over the bow. You may be a person who loves the water and your life is complete only when you are satisfying an inner need to "go down to the sea."

Finally, you may be the operator of a lonely railroad signal tower. In a room high above the rails you are standing before a miniature diagram of the tracks and switches which extend for miles on either

The computer revolution has made the job of these air traffic controllers much easier. (Photo: Delta Air Lines.)

side of you. Tiny, blinking, colored lights show the progress of each train and the position of every signal and switch. It is your responsibility to see that every train operates on the correct track and is cleared to maintain its schedule according to the timetable. You have a sense of power and at the same time are aware of your awesome responsibility. Suddenly a 100-car freight train thunders below you and you realize that you are very much a part of this noisy maelstrom. A way of life, indeed!

Remember, though, that you do not necessarily have to hold down one of these more glamorous jobs. Whatever your position, it can become a way of life for you if you will let it. During those hours when you are at work your life can be purposeful. You can do more than just perform your assigned duties, more than report for work to shuffle papers or keep records. You can make your job a vital link in the long chain of activities which keeps your airline, railroad, bus line, subway, or whatever it may be, operating. In a transportation career, you are important to the success of the company, and you can reap the benefits and pleasures which come from a significant job well done.

Overleaf: Jet liners (above), and ocean liners (below) carry hundreds of passengers. (Photos: Boeing, and *The Eugenio C.* of the Costa Line, and Moran Towing, New York.)

CHAPTER 2

TRANSPORTATION: AN ESSENTIAL INDUSTRY

The three basic human needs are food, clothing, and shelter. Primitive tribes had to derive all of their necessities from what was at hand; but once people were able to travel beyond their tiny primeval villages, they could contact neighbors to exchange goods, and transportation entered the picture.

At first these people carried articles on their backs. Then they probably developed a crude form of travois similar to that used by early American Indians. If there was a river or body of water nearby, they learned to fashion rafts of logs and push or paddle the cargo to its destination. People did not wait for the invention of the wheel to move goods or themselves. In fact, water transport was so effective that most of the world's early great cities sprang from such early villages situated near the ocean or along a river.

Once the wheel was invented and animals were domesticated, however, people devised other and more reliable forms of transportation over land. Water transport had reached a high degree of development before networks of roads appeared, the Romans being the first to appreciate the value of highways both for shipping goods and marching armies to distant lands. With roads to connect them to the outside world, towns could be built inland, but for centuries little progress was made in the carriage of people or goods overland until late in the eighteenth century. By this time lumbering stagecoaches were providing the best transportation devised to date, canals were being dug, and scientists were investigating various ways of harnessing steam's energy in order to put it to work.

American transportation enthusiasts must have enjoyed the nineteenth century! The Lancaster Turnpike, a fine macadam road laid between Philadelphia and Lancaster, was the first good road surface in the young nation. In 1807 Robert Fulton sailed the first commercially successful steamboat on the Hudson River. Meanwhile laborers were digging canals and constructing toll roads so that many parts of the country were becoming accessible for the first time, but when the Baltimore and Ohio Railroad operated its first steam train in 1830, transportation experienced its greatest advance to date. Thereafter rails were pushed in every direction, making the highways of secondary importance until the automobile was mass produced and perfected in the early twentieth century.

Soon the family car, the bus, and the truck replaced the railroad as the prime mover and then the airplane, originally considered a novelty, displaced all other forms of transportation as the fastest and most popular means of travel. In addition, the plane revolutionized the movement of many types of goods including fresh fruits and vegetables which now could be picked one day, flown thousands of miles, and eaten the next morning in a distant country. Airfreight introduced another important change. Industry no longer had to maintain huge, expensive warehouses to stock parts and supplies. Whatever was needed could be flown overnight from the most distant supplier.

Today transportation ranks with agriculture as one of our most important industries. Without the freight train, truck, ship, or plane no goods could move within the country or between nations. Without the airplane, railroad, bus, or taxi, people would be wholly dependent on their automobiles for transportation.

Vehicles of every kind are vital to the nation in peace and wartime. A long strike by the nation's carriers would leave most electric generating plants without fuel, causing the country to suffer devastating blackouts. Since the bulk of our food is transported by plane or truck, supermarket and corner grocery shelves would soon be bare without their daily deliveries.

Consider what would happen to hospitals if there were a general transportation stoppage. Doctors, nurses, and other personnel would have great difficulty reaching the institutions. Supplies of fresh blood, drugs, medicines, and radioactive substances, to say nothing of food, would be unobtainable. Without electricity the hospitals would be unable to function.

Fortunately there never has been a time when transportation was unavailable. Nevertheless, a strike of the nation's airlines, railroads, bus lines, or the major trucking companies quickly shows how important every segment of the industry is to each of us. Congress has been forced to recognize this and has adopted laws designed to avert a national hardship which could result from widespread and crippling transportation strikes.

If you seek further proof of how essential our transportation is to every American, you can drive on any interstate highway around seven o'clock in the evening and watch the endless stream of trucks rumbling from their metropolitan freight terminals. Then visit an airfreight depot and stand by the conveyors as they move huge piles of packages and crates of every size into the cavernous freighters which will shortly take off and wing their loads to distant points for overnight delivery. Don't overlook the railroad yards either. There, long trains are made up nightly for distant destinations while in many parts of the country special coal trains are shuttling back and forth between mines and power plants.

As for the movement of passengers, visit any large railroad terminal served by commuter lines and note the crowd of men and women hurrying for their trains. More impressive still are the throngs at the huge airport terminals like O'Hare in Chicago, Kennedy in New York, or the sprawling terminals in Atlanta, Los Angeles, Dallas-Fort Worth, or Washington. Here, thousands of passengers arrive, depart, and connect from one airline to another as they travel to and from nearby or distant destinations.

When an industrialist decides to locate a factory in a new location, the first question he asks is: "What transportation facilities are nearby?" Similarly, no one would construct an office building unless bus, trolley, or subway lines served the area. An expensive resort hotel will never be built unless there is adequate air service to bring guests from all parts of the world. Thus business and pleasure follow the sounds of the wheels and the whine of the jets.

Independent shippers like UPS have created many new jobs in the transportation industry. (Photo: UPS.)

The transportation business is essential to the well being of each of us. Does it sound challenging? Would you like to be a part of it and prepare for a rewarding career in some part of the industry? If so, this book will reveal the innumerable opportunities which await you.

This woman is one of a growing number of women train engineers.
(Photo: Santa Fe Railway.)

CHAPTER 3

THE TRANSPORTATION
JOB OUTLOOK

When you accept your first job, whatever it may be, you will be joining a labor force estimated between 122 and 128 million people by 1990. The Bureau of Labor Statistics has identified and classified more than thirty thousand different occupations, hundreds of which will be found in the transportation industry. Selecting the right job from so many occupations can be difficult. That is why it is so important to investigate several job opportunities before you make your final decision. Unfortunately it is not always possible to find openings in the career area which is your first choice; therefore, it is wise to have second and third occupational choices as reserves.

In this chapter we will give you an overall picture of the employment outlook for the 1980s. Then we will touch on the principal transportation employment areas and comment on some topics of interest to everyone considering his or her career future.

TOMORROW'S JOBS

Everyone considering a career should investigate the long-term job opportunities it offers. The man who became an expert maker of buggy whips around the turn of the century was doomed to a short career. He failed to see that automobiles were beginning to crowd horses and carriages off the streets. The same is true today of the young man or woman who studies watchmaking. The century-old spring-driven watch is being replaced by the digital timepiece which has no moving parts. The warning is clear: whatever your occupational choice, be sure to investigate its future.

Before we examine your prospects for a transportation career, let's review the overall job market and survey the decade which will end in 1990. We can do this thanks to the United States Department of Labor's Bureau of Labor Statistics. The latest issue of the *Occupational Outlook Handbook, 1982-83 Edition,* was published by the bureau shortly before this book went to press and provides some helpful and interesting information.

It should be remembered that all projections are subject to economic, social, and political changes among other things. A recession can decrease job demand, whereas a war will create more job openings than there are workers to fill them. Congressional appropriations for public works projects or other government spending which stimulates business can create greater employment opportunities. Since forecasts are based on past experience, present trends, and anticipated development, they are not infallible, but they do represent the best available guides and are well worth considering. With that qualification, let's discover what the labor forecasters see for the years ahead.

The American labor force consists of those workers who are looking for jobs and those who have jobs. The labor force is expected to continue its growth during the 1980s, but at a slower rate than in the past. This will mean an improved employment outlook for young people entering the labor market. For the first time in years competition for the so-called "entry jobs" will be down because fewer young people are graduating from schools and colleges now.

Changes in employment will vary widely among industries. Service occupations, included among which are jobs in hotels, barber shops, automobile repair shops, business service operations, hospitals, and nonprofit organizations, will experience the greatest growth. Trade and manufacturing will follow close behind, with finance, real estate, and insurance next in line before transportation, communications and public utilities. (These latter three industries are grouped together into one category.)

Shifts in population will change the demand for and the supply of workers in local job markets. In areas with a growing population, the demand for services such as fire protection, police, water, retail stores, transportation, various repair and personal services, and schools will increase. At the same time there may be more people seeking work in some occupations than there are jobs to absorb them. Local conditions may vary greatly from the Bureau of Labor Statistics forecasts which are done on a national scale. Therefore it is important to carefully investigate the local job market before you travel any distance in search of a position. You will find information about employment opportunities in Chapter 13.

OCCUPATIONAL FORECASTS IN TRANSPORTATION

The Bureau of Labor Statistics divides occupations into four groupings:

1. White-collar occupations—professional and technical, managerial, clerical, and sales jobs.

2. Blue-collar occupations—craft, operative and manual labor jobs. (Operative refers to operating a vehicle or machine.)

3. Service occupations.

4. Farm occupations.

Since transportation requires certain workers from all of these groupings, let's examine the future for each of them.

White-Collar Occupations. Professional and technical workers include many highly trained individuals such as engineers, scientists, airplane pilots, and accountants. Growth is expected for this group.

Clerical workers constitute the largest occupational group and include bookkeepers, accounting clerks, cashiers, secretaries, and typists. Here employment is expected to grow as much as 27 percent even though technological developments in computers, dictating and office machines will enable clerical workers to do more work in less time and will change the skills needed in some jobs. Just the same, continued growth in most clerical occupations is expected. There are a few exceptions, though, in areas you should note. There will be fewer jobs for keypunch operators, stenographers, and airline reservation and ticket agents; these jobs will decline as improved technology reduces the need for workers. At the same time, however, more extensive use of computers will shoot up demand for computer and related operators.

Blue-Collar Occupations. Requirements for craft workers in the railroad industry will diminish, especially for railroad and car shop repairers. On the other hand, consider the prospects for transport operatives. They include those who drive buses, trucks, taxis, and forklifts, as well as sailors and parking lot attendants. It is expected that in most of these occupations employment will increase by 18 to 26 percent because of the greater use of most types of transportation equipment.

In the manual labor category, the need for freight handlers is expected to grow slowly because power-driven machinery will gradually replace manual workers. It should be remembered, though, that machinery will not replace all labor. Men and women will always be needed for certain jobs which machines, even robots, cannot perform.

Service Occupations. These jobs cover a wide range of activities, but we are concerned only with protective services (security guards), food and beverage preparation (in restaurants, coffee shops, and meal kitchens at airports and other terminals), and personal service occupations which include airplane flight attendants, porters, stewards and stewardesses on buses and ships.

Inasmuch as there are many occasions when airlines, railroads, and ships must feed their passengers and crews, various food service openings will be found in these companies. It is obvious that cleaning and maintenance employees are needed by transportation operators to service the planes, trains, ships, buses, and other vehicles, as well as to clean and maintain passenger and freight terminals and repair shops.

Farm Occupations. Farm output will continue to increase but the employment of farm workers will decline. Actually agriculture offers little for the transportation-minded young person. One can obtain employment driving tractors and other vehicles on large farms, and trucking companies which specialize in hauling milk and other farm products need drivers, but there are no other job opportunities in this field.

It might be said that transportation offers something for everyone interested in seeking a career in this industry. For college graduates and those with graduate degrees, there are management and engineering openings. For those with associate degrees or certificates earned at vocational schools or community colleges, opportunities abound. Even young men and women who want to enter the labor force after graduating from high school can find entry level jobs— positions in the mail department, as building custodians, as manual laborers, in basic clerical jobs, and aircraft, bus, or train cleaners. Whatever your abilities and educational level, you should be able to carve a niche for yourself somewhere in the transportation field.

THE OUTLOOK FOR TRANSPORTATION

Between 1970 and 1980, employment in the transportation, communications, and public utilities sector increased only a third as fast as in the service industries. This was due to the declining needs of railroad and water transportation companies.

Employment in the sector as a whole is expected to rise by a million to a million and a half workers between 1980 and 1990. Although the number of employees required by rail and water transport companies will continue to decline, you will find that air, local transit, and trucking will experience the greatest growth. Employment as a whole in transportation will rise by between 12 to 18 percent from 3,600,000 to around 4,300,000 workers.

As we shall see in the chapters which follow, the demand for workers will vary greatly from one type of transportation service to another. Before considering occupational prospects, however, it would be well to comment briefly on your educational background, the new employment opportunities for women, and the role of unions in transportation.

WHAT ABOUT YOUR EDUCATIONAL BACKGROUND?

The educational attainment of our nation's labor force has risen from an average of 11.1 years of school in 1952 to 12.7 years in 1980.

Many technical, craft, and office occupations now require vocational education or an apprenticeship following high school. On the whole, you will find that employers prefer to hire trained workers rather than train them. (Airline stewardesses are an exception in the transportation field.)

Although traditionally a college education has been looked upon as a guarantee of success, reality has not borne this out. That is because those occupations which demand college training have not expanded fast enough to absorb the growing supply of college graduates. This has been especially true in professional, technical, and managerial occupations which did not grow enough to absorb the expanding supply of college graduates. Between 1969 and 1978, one out of every four college graduates had to accept a job which was not appropriate for his or her education and abilities. As for the future, it appears that more college graduates will visit employment agencies than are needed to fill those job openings which call for their degrees. Not all occupations will be overcrowded, however. The Bureau of Labor Statistics anticipates that engineers, programmers, and systems analysts will be in very strong demand.

Don't let this discourage you from going to college or remaining in college if you are presently an undergraduate. If you have a college degree, you will have a better chance of obtaining employment and holding the best paying managerial and professional jobs. You must not give up plans for pursuing a career you think will match your interests and abilities, but you should be aware of the job market conditions and limitations you may encounter.

Since a high school diploma is now the minimum standard requirement for almost any job, it is vital that you complete your education at least through the twelfth grade. High school dropouts find it increasingly difficult to obtain jobs; the wise young man or woman is able to produce that all-important diploma when talking with a personnel interviewer.

OPPORTUNITIES FOR WOMEN

Prior to World War II, few people would have accepted the idea that a woman could be a truck driver, dispatch airplanes, or even command a Coast Guard cutter. Until 1942, women worked mostly in clerical occupations, in the garment industry, and in some light manufacturing plants; they dominated the nursing profession and served as maids and cooks in private homes, hotels, and hospitals.

The tremendous manpower needs of World War II broke down prejudice against hiring women in many industries, especially in defense plants. "Rosie the Riveter" became the popular nickname for women workers in factories where they worked side by side with men, putting in long hours and taking on tough manual assignments previously performed only by men. Even the military services recruited women to work in office jobs and other non-combatant positions.

Once the war was over, some women returned to their homes and families but many remained in their jobs. Since that time, the demand for equal rights has resulted in the federal government's affirmative action program. This provides that employers who wish to bid on federal contracts must draw up and put into practice plans for hiring and promoting women and members of minority groups. Today women are supposed to receive equal pay with men for performing the same jobs. They are also being hired for many positions which were previously closed to them because of their sex.

A recent survey of top executives revealed that many of the traditional prejudices against women managers are disappearing. The study found that women executives are performing on the job as well or better than expected and that they are making significant contributions to their companies. Although it will be several years before you can aspire to a management position, if you are a woman, you can be quite certain that you will receive equal consideration with men for advancement to a supervisory or management post, assuming you have the necessary qualifications.

UNIONIZATION IN THE TRANSPORTATION INDUSTRY

One of the first recorded instances of workers forming a union occurred in Philadelphia during 1792 when a group of shoemaker journeymen formed an association to better their working conditions. These early unionists would never have considered banding together for their common good if their employers had treated them fairly. It can be said quite truthfully that unions would not have been necessary if managers had not exploited their employees. Unfortunately there are still some businesses where the working conditions might be intolerable were it not for the unions which represent the employees and negotiate contracts on behalf of their members.

The majority of employees in transportation belong to unions. Where a union shop is in effect an employer is free to hire union or nonunion workers, but all new employees must join the union within a certain time limit, usually thirty days. Each such employee must also continue to pay dues to the union for the duration of the union contract.

Airline pilots, among the highest paid employees in every company, are unionized, and in some companies even the office workers belong to unions. If you wish to work in this industry at a job covered by a union contract, you should be prepared to join a union. Should you have doubts about wanting to do this, you either should seek another job not covered by a union contract or rethink your position.

As you read ahead, you will meet Joe Curran who organized the National Maritime Union and learn why he felt it necessary to do this. Most of the unions which represent transport workers have been able to win many benefits for their members in addition to pay increases. Newspapers play up strikes and labor violence, but they occur less frequently than is commonly thought. Harmonious relations exist between employees and employers in most companies and as a union member you will enjoy certain protections and benefits in return for your dues.

Although unions have been able to obtain large wage increases for their members, some settlements have been considered excessively generous, especially if they were more than company earnings could justify. However, in the early 1980s many unions became ready to modify their demands for increased wages and benefits. In some cases, union negotiators even agreed to no increases or pay cuts in order to keep their transport companies solvent and retain their members' jobs.

Why, you may well ask, if transportation is such an essential industry, would there be no pay increases and possible cuts? The reason, as will be explained in later chapters, is that deregulation changed the whole way of doing business in the airline and trucking industries. Furthermore, with the whole country in an economic recession during the early 1980s, most businesses were forced to cut back. With fewer people employed and with consumers spending less money, it was inevitable that factories were making fewer shipments and many people were unable to travel. Transportation companies reduced their services somewhat but they were still very much alive and far healthier than the steel, copper, automobile, and lumber industries, to mention a few. Although the number of employees may expand or contract, transportation will remain an essential industry, well worth considering for your life's work.

Therefore, as you read ahead, have paper and pencil handy so you can make notes about any career opportunities which seem especially appealing. List the advantages and disadvantages of the work as well as the reasons why you think you would or would not be suited for it. Then when you reach Chapter 13, which discusses how to choose a job, you will have data to help you make some decisions.

Let's start our career survey with a look at the bus industry which carries more passengers and serves more cities and towns in the United States than any other form of transportation.

Overleaf: Many people rely on buses to get to out-of-the way places where train or plane transportation is impractical. (Photo: Greyhound Lines, Inc.)

CHAPTER 4

THE INTERCITY
PEOPLE MOVERS

If you have a good atlas, you will find the little mining town of Hibbing, Minnesota in the northeastern part of the state. Hibbing's chief claim to fame is probably that it is the birthplace of the giant Greyhound Corporation which today operates more than 4,400 buses over a hundred thousand miles of routes in the United States, Alaska, Canada, and Mexico.

In 1914, horse-drawn vehicles provided most of the transportation in Hibbing except for a few livery autos which were rented at five dollars an hour. Carl Wickman, who had recently emigrated from Sweden, owned one of the delivery cars. He had opened an auto agency, but when his one car didn't sell, he had to do something with the Hupmobile, so he put it out to hire.

One day he had an inspiration. People were always traveling back and forth between Hibbing and nearby Alice. Wickman decided to operate his car hourly on a regular schedule between these two towns. The day after he began, he made a sign and started his little one-man, one-vehicle, bus line. Folks soon knew they could catch his car in front of the saloon in Hibbing and fifteen minutes later get off at the firehouse at Alice. The fare was fifteen cents one way, twenty-five cents round trip. Soon passengers not only filled the car but clung to the running boards and fenders.

Seeing Wickman's success, one of his competitors, Ralph Bogan, decided to operate over the same route at the same rates. Wickman's business fell off when he had to share it with Bogan and a price war followed until Wickman suggested that instead of fighting each other, they join forces. Bogan agreed and the new partners combined their capital and equipment. Soon they were building more buses and extending their operations south until they reached the city of Minneapolis.

At the time that the partners were pushing their little bus line farther out of Hibbing, Wickman met another young man who had been an auto mechanic, owned an auto agency, and was now operating a bus line running out of Superior, Wisconsin. Wickman persuaded Orville S. Caesar to join forces with Bogan and himself, and thereafter the three embarked on a steady program of buying up bus lines, integrating them into their existing operation, and at the same time steadily extending their routes in all directions.

Nothing stopped them during these busy years of growth in the early 1920s. They hopped over state lines, pushed across rivers, and conquered the highest mountain ranges, constantly pushing out into new territories. The only barriers Wickman, Bogan, and Caesar acknowledged were the Atlantic and Pacific oceans and the Mexican border (because there were no good roads beyond that point). During this period the trio called their business the Motor Transit Company, although some of its bus lines operated under more colorful names.

It was from one of the little lines, a company in western Michigan which had joined up with Wickman and his associates, that the Greyhound name came. A sketch of a racing greyhound was painted on the side of each bus and patrons referred to it as "the Greyhound line." The name appealed to Wickman and the others as singularly appropriate and it was adopted quickly for the entire system. That was in 1926.

Greyhound, like all forms of transportation, suffered a serious loss of traffic during the Depression. Money was so tight that few people could afford to travel. To Wickman and the other members of management this situation offered a challenge, for they were convinced that people would ride their buses if they were offered inexpensive but comfortable traveling conditions. Buses had come a long way from those first homemade affairs Wickman and Bogan had built. As they grew larger and more comfortable, various technical problems had to be solved. Caesar, for instance, had invented the first hot-water heater for buses, thus ending the dangerous practice of heating via the exhaust pipe with its treacherous carbon monoxide gas.

Snowstorms often delayed or blocked buses until the company developed a truck-driven snowplow of a type still in use today. The management constantly worked on plans for roomier and better buses that would carry more passengers. In 1934 the first engine-in-the-rear, integral-type bus appeared, and two years later, Greyhound operated its first air-conditioned bus. In 1938 diesel engines were adopted as standard equipment on the fleet. As early as 1940 plans were made for a revolutionary new bus, the Scenicruiser, but due to the war, it was not until 1954 that this forty-foot, double-decker bus with washroom facilities, twin diesels, air suspension and other comforts appeared on the nation's high-ways.

The same year the Scenicruiser appeared, Wickman died, leaving Caesar as president and Bogan as executive vice president. For thirty years these men had worked together and nurtured their baby until it attained the maturity and status of a major corporation. No longer was it owned by the original trio but by more than sixty thousand stockholders. With pride the company called itself "the world's largest passenger transportation company," but in spite of this boast and its size, all was not well.

The company had stopped growing at a time when the nation's economy was steadily expanding. Profits were falling off in ten of the Greyhound operating companies. Obviously the time had come for the two remaining founders to take a back seat and give the wheel to a younger trouble shooter who had imagination, energy and ability to make the company tick again. Consultants hired by the board of directors recommended they hire a competent outsider who would clean up the trouble and bring in some fresh ideas to the organization. Arthur S. Genet, vice president of the Chesapeake and Ohio Railroad, was selected as the man best qualified to do the job. On his arrival Caesar stepped up to chairman of the board and Genet was elected president and chief executive officer effective January 1, 1956.

Genet spent his first six weeks traveling. He visited the headquarters of the ten operating companies, talked with the operating presidents, met key personnel, and inspected their facilities. Once back in headquarters in Chicago, he arranged to have all supervisory personnel, except the operating presidents, take aptitude tests. Then he met with each of the presidents, reviewed the results and actual performance records of each man tested, and together they decided whom they would replace. A total of 259 men were dismissed and Genet observed regretfully that this was the most distasteful thing he ever had to do.

One of the presidents under Genet said that it was a job that should never have had to be done. He went on to explain that none of the men who was dismissed should have been advanced to such high positions in the first place but that in many cases friendship played a big role.

To rebuild employee morale, which suffered from such a wholesale cutting out of management, Genet insisted that all replacements be filled from the ranks. There was only one exception, a financial specialist. Genet's next move was to establish a training program so that approximately 200 top supervisory personnel could be thoroughly indoctrinated in sound management philosophy. These men were to attend one of three universities where special courses were established just for them.

At the same time, Genet, who felt that the presidents of the operating companies were unnecessarily restricted in what they could do, drew up plans to decentralize the company. The performance of each bus operating division was to be entirely the responsibility of its president.

Step number one to fill the buses, was to go after the people who make business and pleasure trips. Ads aimed at drivers of private cars were designed to win them over to Greyhound for intercity travel.

"It's such a comfort to take the bus—and leave the driving to us," was the text of a singing jingle used extensively. For 1957, Genet's goal was to add one passenger to each schedule.

Greyhound all-expense tours were introduced to attract vacation travelers to events such as the Rose Bowl football game, the Mardi Gras, and other festivals. The first land-sea trip to Hawaii via

Greyhound and Matson Navigation Company sold out quickly. Next, Genet met with railroad executives who were anxious to get rid of their unprofitable passenger business, particularly on branch lines. Genet was eager to substitute his buses for short- or long-haul railroad service, except commuting service which is never profitable.

Genet turned his sights on other kinds of transportation also. It may seem odd, for example, that Genet looked to airline passengers as a good source of business, but consider the situation in Detroit. Airline travelers must take a thirty-five-mile ride on Greyhound to get from the Willow Run Airport to downtown Detroit. Genet found that other airports of major cities were also situated far from the downtown area.

In addition to the above-mentioned expansions, Genet decided it was illogical to think of a bus as capable of carrying only passengers. Why not also haul small packages, newspapers and the like in the roomy baggage compartments under each bus, he thought? As a result of this thinking, Greyhound now offers its Greyhound Package Express, including pickup and delivery service in more than 260 cities in 38 states.

When Gerald Troutman took over the wheel as chairman in 1966, he drove the company down the expansion road taking it to a place among the nation's top 100 corporations. One of his first moves was to acquire Armour, the giant of the meat packing industry, and then move the company headquarters to Phoenix, Arizona. One company led to another and today computers, equipment leasing, insurance and banking are but some of the company businesses. In fact, it has been said that if you took a cross-country trip on a Greyhound bus you would pay for your trip with Greyhound money orders, insure your luggage with Greyhound insurance, eat Armour products at Greyhound fast food restaurants, wash with Dial soap, and if you were to look up at the sky, you would possibly see some of the jet aircraft the company owns or leases.

But to return to the bus operation and get some idea of the scope of the transport activities, the company has approximately 18,000 employees, including 8,400 drivers for the company's fleet of 4,400 buses. Every day the fleet serves nearly 14,000 locations, compared with 650 served by scheduled airlines and some 525 by Amtrak. As the largest manufacturer of intercity buses in North America, Greyhound adds an average of one new bus to its fleet every day.

Greyhound has come a long way since that first trip Carl Wickman made in his Hupmobile. From carrying a few dozen passengers a day in 1912, the Greyhound Corporation has become the largest intercity carrier of passengers in the nation, hauling nearly 64 million men, women, and children during a recent year!

A LOOK AT THE BUS INDUSTRY

Buses provide many communities with their only means of public transportation to and from the outside world. Those who live in large cities may find that the bus is a convenient alternative to air and rail travel. In fact, over short distances such as between Boston and Providence, or New York and Philadelphia, your bus may prove almost as fast as a plane or train and the service may be more frequent. Bus terminals are usually located in the heart of the city, whereas the railroad station may not be as convenient.

To understand the bus industry it would be helpful to have a picture of the larger carriers, those 1,330 companies which operate between cities, and which are known as intercity carriers.

The Interstate Commerce Commission (ICC) requires all bus operators which cross state lines to obtain an ICC operating certificate. The Commission classifies interstate bus companies in two categories:

1. *Class I Operators*—companies which have annual revenues of $3 million or more. In 1980 there were forty-six such companies which did 90 percent of the regularly-scheduled intercity bus service.

2. *Other Interstate Carriers*—companies which do less than $3 million worth of business each year.

In addition, there are those bus lines which provide intrastate service (operate wholly within one state) and companies which offer charter or other special services to the public. These latter operators carry about 67 percent of this type of business.

Unlike other forms of transportation, which need to maintain stations or terminals with a number of workers at each stop where passengers board or leave their planes or trains, buses are uniquely able to eliminate this expense in most of the communities they serve. The corner garage, drug, or paper store serves as a waiting room for passengers, and the owner sells tickets and provides travel information. These arrangements cut down on the number of employees required to operate a rural bus system.

Greyhound is the largest bus carrier. Second in line is Trailways, Inc., and there are approximately 1,330 other companies which make up the intercity bus industry in the United States. If you are a reader who enjoys statistics, here are a few for you: these bus companies operate twenty-two thousand vehicles, employ some fifty thousand men and women, and during a recent year carried 373 million passengers. This fleet serves some fifteen thousand places listed in the *Official Bus Guide* and many others not listed there. In fact, all the airlines and railroads serve less than a thousand of the cities and towns where buses arrive and depart daily. Little wonder buses are America's most familiar form of transportation and that between 1979 and 1980 bus travel increased while fewer passengers rode the airlines and Amtrak. Buses are big business, a $2 billion business, for that is the amount of money intercity ticket sellers collected during 1980. And this figure does not include the charter companies.

Of the forty-six larger intercity carriers which are all Class I operators, Greyhound carried almost 50 percent of the passengers. Trailways served the next largest number, and the other forty-four companies divided up what was left. As for employees, 60 percent of all those working for Class I carriers received their paychecks from Greyhound.

"All right," you may well say, "now what do all these statistics mean?"

It does not take a mathematical genius to realize that apart from the two leaders in the industry, Greyhound and Trailways, the other companies offer limited employment opportunities. Openings would be mostly for clerical positions, some ticket agents, mechanics to service and repair the vehicles, cleaners, and perhaps a few custodians if the bus line operated its own terminal. Openings will vary according to the size of a company and the complexity of its operations. The very largest operators might offer additional employment possibilities for dispatchers, computer specialists, accountants, and applicants with an economics and/or statistical background. These last two specialties might qualify applicants as forecasters, rate and schedule specialists, and financial analysts. So-called professionals, public relations specialists, attorneys, and business librarians, would find little or no real opportunity.

Since the business of hauling passengers by bus is uncomplicated, a small company can operate profitably with a half dozen buses, a few drivers, and as many other employees needed to keep the books, sell tickets, and service the vehicles. For most companies it is a "bus and driver" business. The driver is the most important employee in the business because he or she is the operator of the bus and to the passenger that person is the company. Half of Greyhound's employees are drivers; therefore, if you would like to enter this industry and enjoy driving, give careful consideration to the possibility of becoming a driver.

NATURE OF THE WORK

What would you do on the first day you report for work? You have completed your training and are proudly wearing your new uniform as an important member of the company team.

Upon arriving at the garage or terminal where you are assigned a bus, you pick up tickets, report forms, and other items needed for your trip. Then you find your bus and inspect the vehicle to make certain that the steering mechanism, brakes, windshield wipers, lights and mirrors are working properly. Then you check the fuel, water, oil, tires, and see that the necessary safety equipment is on board. This includes first aid kits, fire extinguishers, and emergency reflectors.

Your inspection completed, you drive to the loading dock and if there is no porter to help load the baggage, you stand near the door to collect tickets, check bags, and store them in the luggage compartment. You might use the terminal's public address system to announce the destination, route, time of departure and arrival at the next stop, and other information. At last the departure time has come and you settle into your seat, turn on the ignition switch, and off you go.

If yours is a local run, you probably will stop at many small towns only a few miles apart. At each stop you help passengers leave and board the bus, unload and load baggage, and take tickets. If it is an express run, you will probably drive several hours on an interstate or other highway before making your first stop. En route you will regulate the lighting, heating, and air-conditioning equipment. Should you get a flat or something goes wrong with the engine, it is your job to change the tire and if possible fix the motor, should repair service not be available.

At your destination, you discharge your passengers, drive the bus to the garage, or turn it over to the next driver and then prepare your reports. The US Department of Transportation requires drivers keep a record of each trip. The following is recorded: distance traveled, periods of time off duty, and time spent performing other duties. You also must report any repairs or special servicing the bus might need, and it is possible that your employer expects you to complete certain company reports as well.

If you drive a chartered bus, you pick up a group of people, take them to whatever destination is set on the schedule, and remain with them until they are ready to return. Some charter buses are used for organized tours in which case you would stay away from home for one or more nights.

Should you drive an intercity bus, you can expect to work at all hours of the day and night, every day of the year. As a new driver you will be on call at all hours and may have to report for work at short notice. If you are away from home overnight there will be a meal allowance and possibly reimbursement of your hotel expense. Driving schedules range from six to ten hours a day and from 3¼ to 6 days a week, but under US Department of Transportation regulations you cannot, as an intercity driver, drive more than ten hours without at least eight consecutive hours off. Although driving is not physically difficult, it is tiring and calls for steady nerves. You alone are responsible for the safety of your passengers and bus and that calls for an alert mind.

GREYHOUND REQUIREMENTS

Here is what the Greyhound Corporation expects of its applicants:

1. Applicants must be between twenty-four and thirty-five years of age.
2. Applicants must have at least 20/40 vision with or without corrective lens.
3. Applicants must pass the Greyhound preemployment physical examination; applicants must have weight proportionate to height to be determined by the company doctor.
4. Applicants must have no more than two moving violations and/or accidents in the last three years and no suspension or revocation within the last three years. They must have no more than four moving violations and/or accidents in the last five years or one suspension or revocation within the last five years.
5. Applicants must meet all applicable federal and state requirements.
6. Applicants must have an acceptable employment record and demonstrate mature judgment and good character.

To become a bus driver you must successfully complete Greyhound's driver training school. Prior experience as a bus driver is not required.

Long before it became the popular thing to do, Greyhound had been an equal opportunity employer. Through the years, not only has Greyhound insisted on fair and equal treatment of minority groups using its service, but has tried to insure the same impartiality regarding employment in the company.

It should be emphasized, however, that Greyhound hires drivers only *once during the year,* in early spring. Employment inquiries should be directed to your local Greyhound Company operated terminal.

A FEW OTHER IMPORTANT FACTS

It should be noted that in some companies those drivers with low seniority may be laid off temporarily during the winter when traffic drops. Most intercity drivers belong to one of three unions: The Amalgamated Transit Union, the United Transportation Union, or the International Brotherhood of Teamsters. In 1980 drivers for large intercity bus companies earned an average annual salary of about $22,000, a wage about 75 percent above the average for all nonsupervisory workers in private industry, except farmers. Wages are computed either on a mileage basis or, for short runs, on an hourly rate. Most drivers are guaranteed a minimum number of miles or hours per pay period.

For the addresses of local bus companies, see the yellow pages in your phone directory. You can find the names and addresses of most bus companies and get an idea of the size of each by looking in the *Motor Coach Guide.* If this is unavailable at a local bus station, travel agency, or public library, contact your state employment service for assistance.

Overleaf: Jobs with airlines vary greatly in the types of skills and training required. (Photo: Delta Air Lines.)

CHAPTER 5

AN AIRLINE CAREER

The silvery Boeing 747 disappeared into a puffy cloud and as it emerged into the clear the captain switched on the microphone.

"Ladies and gentlemen," said the voice. "May I have your attention, please. This is Captain Warren. We are about to start our descent from 40,000 feet and we will be landing in Boston in about 25 minutes. In contrast to the warm California weather which we left a short time ago, snow has been falling for about an hour, but the runway is clear and we will have no problem landing. We are estimating we will be two minutes ahead of schedule. The temperature at the airport is presently 20 degrees. For your comfort may I suggest that you remain in your seats and prepare to fasten your seat belts. Thank you."

Immediately the stewards and stewardesses started hurrying up and down the aisles, collecting the dinner trays and coffee cups. Once the dishes were stored in the galley, two of them began to take coats to the passengers, noting the seat numbers of each on tags fastened to the buttons. By the time the "Fasten Seat Belt" signs glowed, all of the clothing had been distributed and two of the stewardesses were walking slowly up the aisle checking to see that all of the passengers had fastened their belts.

"Ladies and gentlemen," the familiar voice said, "this is your captain again. Please observe the "No-Smoking" sign as we are now preparing for our final approach and landing. You may not be able to see through the snowflakes which are falling outside, but your flight crew has a clear electronic view of our flight path. We will be on the ground in about three minutes. Thank you."

Six minutes later the plane came to a gentle stop as it nudged against the terminal dock. A moment later the cabin door was open and the first passengers were departing. As soon as the cabin was empty, a crew of cleaners entered and began their job of making it ready for the next flight.

"I'm new on this job," one of the women said to another worker. "Where does this plane go next?"

"Leaves in an hour and a half for St. Louis. Doesn't give us much time to do our job. We have to be finished within half an hour. But I'll tell you something, when a plane's late, then we *really* have to hustle. That dispatcher wants every plane cleared on time for departure."

Meanwhile, up in the dispatcher's office a new crew was arriving and getting ready to board the plane. The two pilots and a flight engineer were leaning over a map table and conferring with Ellen Martin, the dispatcher. She looked up and frowned.

"You're going to have some tough going, getting off the ground if this snow keeps up," she warned. "Better make sure the wings are clear; it's really coming down now."

"Don't worry, we won't take off it there's any question of safety," the older of the two pilots replied.

Meanwhile a mechanic had gone into the cockpit to check the aircraft log and see if there were any irregularities which the captain on the incoming flight had recorded. He noted the entry: "Check stabilizers—working sluggish." The young man immediately started to check out the cables which ran beneath the cabin floor to the rear wings and soon discovered that one of the loops through which the heavy wire passed was not properly adjusted. Other mechanics were making normal inspections while a huge gasoline truck was refueling the wing tanks. The driver shivered in the storm as he held the heavy hose. A food service truck had driven up to the rear cabin door where men were removing the soiled dinner trays and dishes. Once this was done another truck arrived with the meals and beverage service for the outgoing flight.

In a departure lounge in one of the airport concourse wings which extend from the main terminal building, two passenger service representatives in trim, dark brown uniforms were standing at the desk. They were taking tickets from arriving passengers, assigning them seats, and answering their questions.

"Yes, ma'am, we expect the flight to depart on time."

"No, there should be no problem with the weather, Mr. Bain. The snowplows are clearing the runway and the snow will be removed from the wings just before takeoff. Once the plane is airborne you'll quickly rise above this weather. You should have a pleasant flight."

The pilots and the flight engineer were still studying the latest weather maps and talking with the dispatcher. "Look," she said, "there's no good weather to the west between here and Pittsburgh. Your best bet is to fly directly south to Baltimore and skirt the storm there; then go due west. See how the center of the storm is moving?" The captain nodded in agreement. "Get upstairs to about 36,000 feet as fast as you can, and you shouldn't have any trouble."

An hour later a flight attendant swung the massive cabin door shut and locked it. The first officer turned on the engines and the plane slowly left the terminal. It turned and soon disappeared from view in the snow as it taxied to the end of the runway.

"Flight 82, get ready for takeoff," the tower operator ordered over the radio.

"Roger," the captain replied.

"Flight 82 cleared for takeoff."

The first officer applied full power and as the captain released the brakes the aircraft started down the long runway. Forty seconds later it was fully airborne and on its way to St. Louis.

To Ellen Martin, this was just one more regular scheduled takeoff.

This account of a routine flight gives the impression that airlines always offer dependable and steady employment, and that schedules go along daily without a hitch. This is not entirely true. Unlike a train which must follow steel rails, buses and trucks which must stay on highways, and ships which can only sail on the water, airplanes can fly in any direction to any part of the world. Nevertheless, this freedom, as we shall see, invites unlimited competition which can lead to chaos.

AIR TRANSPORTATION—AN UP AND DOWN BUSINESS

On May 13, 1982, passengers were strapped in their seat belts waiting for the Braniff plane to take off when the stewardess made an announcement.

"I have been asked to tell you that Braniff is suspending all operations." Her voice was full of emotion. "Therefore, will all passengers kindly leave the cabin. We are not going to operate this flight." The young woman turned away from the microphone and sobbed, because she, as well as some five thousand other employees, were suddenly without jobs. It was almost impossible to believe. One minute they were ready to take off for their regular scheduled flight to Atlanta and the next, everything had fallen apart. Without warning, there was no company, no job, no more flying.

This tragic incident is recounted not to discourage you from seeking an airline career, but to show that air transportation has its good and bad times, its advantages and drawbacks. Actually, the airlines have expanded and contracted their operations in the past like an accordion. However, in 1982, the changes were more extreme. For the first time, a major carrier had shut down altogether. At the same time American Airlines announced that lack of business had forced it to suspend service to Columbus, Ohio, and Louisville, Kentucky, two cities it had served for over half a century. Much worse were the stories circulating that the globe-circling giant, Pan American World Airways, was in serious trouble, and could become a second Braniff. What was wrong? What had happened to cause these problems?

Not only had fuel costs skyrocketed, but the nation's economy had started to sag and then spun into a recession in 1981. That same year a strike by the Professional Air Traffic Controllers Organization caused the industry great harm. The federal government fired all strikers who did not return to work by a deadline set by the President. Thereafter all airlines were forced to cut their schedules because fewer traffic controllers were manning the control towers. The airlines carried fewer pasengers due to the recession and were forced to cut scheduled trips because of the controllers. This was not the entire story, however.

From 1938 to 1978 the nation's airlines were regulated by the Civil

Aeronautics Board (CAB). The CAB decided the routes each company could fly, the fares it could charge, and regulated many other aspects of the business. In 1978 Congress enacted a law which deregulated the airlines and in effect gave them and all newcomers freedom to fly where they chose and to charge whatever they wished with certain limitations.

The immediate result of this law was that many new companies sprang up giving tough competition to the older carriers and forcing them to reduce their rates and change their routes. As fares kept falling, so did profits, until most of the companies were operating in the red. Thus what had once been a generally thriving industry was now reporting one deficit after another. Employees received layoff notices, schedules were cut, services discontinued, and airplanes parked at the far end of airports. One bad report followed another but the picture was not altogether black.

Airline managements were taking a fresh look at their businesses and coming up with new ideas. One of the most important was a concept which revolutionized parts of the traditional airline route pattern. It was called "hub and spoke", which was simple and could work well for some carriers.

For example, instead of flying five planes directly from New York to Atlanta, Birmingham, Jacksonville, Mobile, and St. Petersburg, an airline would fly from New York only to Atlanta—the hub. There, other local planes, the spokes, would be scheduled for each of the other cities. The system is not as convenient for passengers because they must change planes but it reduces the number of trips and saves money. For some carriers the concept has great advantages.

Another new development brought on by deregulation has been the appearance of many small commuter airlines like Tennessee Airways which offers much needed short haul service along with employment opportunities. Stuart Adcock was not only Tennessee's president, principal stockholder, and head pilot, but also its chief window washer. He would pilot a flight from Nashville to Knoxville, and the instant the plane was empty he would clean the cabin, empty ashtrays, and wipe the windows.

He felt that a prerequisite for employment was a genuine enjoyment of work and the attitude that everyone did whatever work needed to be done.

The company employed forty men and women, eighteen of whom were pilots. Salaries were far below those paid elsewhere in the industry but the company grew. Like some of the other 200 commuter lines, Adcock's had no flight attendants, served no food, and even had no bathroom. He observed that deregulation produced a kind of "gas war" atmosphere in airline operations. A success like Adcock's is bound to attract competitors, but that is what free enterprise is all about, especially under deregulation.

The really good news is that airlines provide essential transportation. Although individual companies may merge with others or even fail, planes will continue to fly. What this tells us is that if you are thinking of seeking an airline career, if possible you should investigate before approaching a company for a job. Avoid the weak carriers if you can, and concentrate your job search on the stronger lines. Obviously if you live in an area served by one or two airlines you have little choice, but should you be in a large city where several carriers fly in and out of the airport, you can be a little more selective perhaps. If you know anyone who works for an airline or at an airport, talk with her or him; ask an older friend of the family who is in business to advise you, or consult one of the financial services which give up to date information about air transportation companies. Visit a nearby bank or a brokerage firm and explain your reason for wanting to see such reports. You should find people willing to help you.

Since airlines are here to stay, they must have people to run them and many will continue to offer career opportunities to interested young men and women. The nature of the business makes it in some ways the most complicated in the transportation industry and therefore one with the greatest number of different jobs. Many call for specialized training. For the purpose of reviewing the employment opportunities within the brief space available here, let's divide the business into two broad categories: airline operations, and airline management. A quick visit to each area of a typical larger airline will give you an idea of some of the positions you may want to consider. All jobs mentioned on the following pages will call for at least a high school education. If additional education or training is required, that will be mentioned.

OPERATING THE AIRLINE

Passenger Service Personnel

The first airline employee to greet us as we arrive at the terminal is a skycap who loads our luggage on a hand cart and follows us to the ticket counter. Here the passenger service representative, a woman in a tailored blue uniform who was recently promoted from the ticket counter, leads us to a ticket agent who examines our tickets and assigns us seats. Then the agent weighs our luggage and places it on a conveyor belt which whisks it to the baggage room. The service representative has either received special in-service training, or was promoted from the reservations department, and is fully familiar with everything that goes on at the airport.

Ramp Service Employees

While waiting for our flight we obtain permission to go downstairs to observe the numerous ramp service employees, those all-important men and women who perform the innumerable ground duties necessary to keep the airline flying. It is they who swarm over and through an airplane when it has completed its trip and must be cleaned and serviced for its next flight. It is they who lift the baggage off the conveyor, sort it and place it on the various carts, each marked for a different departure. They also unload baggage from incoming planes and see that it reaches the baggage claim room where passengers locate and retrieve their own luggage. It is they who load and unload mail, freight, and express. Finally, it is they who drive the food service trucks, mechanized equipment, and the fuel trucks as well as assist with fueling the aircraft.

A ramp service employee, assigned to driving the various pieces of equipment, must have a driver's license and in some cases a chauffeur's license too. Those who handle luggage, express, and freight should also be in good health and have the physical strength needed to lift heavy bags and boxes.

Mechanics

Other employees who are vital to airline efficiency and safety are the mechanics who have a low profile compared to those performing ramp service duties. We see a mechanic peering up into the fuselage of a Boeing 707 while another is replacing a hydraulic line which retracts the landing gear. Airline mechanics have one or two ratings: an airframe rating (referring to the body of the airplane) or a power plant rating (referring to the engine). Most of them have both ratings or licenses which they obtain from the Federal Aviation Administration after successfully passing an examination. To take the test an applicant must have had at least eighteen months' experience for each license (thirty months' experience for both licenses), or have graduated from an approved aviation mechanic's training school.

You can gain this all-important license in one of three ways:

1. *On-the-job training.* A few people become mechanics who have had experience in automobile repair work or other mechanical work by learning while working.
2. *Training in the armed forces.* Those who were aircraft mechanics in one of the military services usually have earned credit toward work experience and other requirements for the license.
3. *Training in a school certified by the Federal Aviation Administration.* This is the route most men and women take who hope to become airline mechanics. The minimum amount of time required to complete the course is 1,150 hours for an airframe rating; 1,150 hours for a power plant rating; and 1,900 hours for both ratings. Before taking the FAA examination you must prove you have had at least eighteen months' work experience for each license (thirty months' work experience for both licenses), or graduation from an approved aviation mechanic's training school. In addition you must be at least 18 years of age and able to read, write, and speak English. For a list of approved Aviation Maintenance Technical Training Schools and information about training facilities, tuition, available financing and other data, write: Career, Aviation Maintenance Foundation, P.O. Box 739, Basin, Wyoming 82410.

Operations Office Employees

We duck into the offices which line the ramp, their large windows affording those working indoors a good view of all the aircraft as well as those employees who are servicing, repairing, or loading them. A quick walk down an aisle enables us to glance into the various offices, the first of which is that of the station manager. As the title suggests he is the overall administrator responsible for the entire company operation at the airport. He has earned this assignment after several years spent in various positions, perhaps starting his career as an aircraft cleaner.

Flight Dispatcher

Next to his office is that of the flight dispatcher, in this case a young woman who determines how each plane can reach its destination on time at the least operating cost, but with the maximum load of passengers and cargo. She must take into consideration such things as the temperature, the amount of fuel loaded, number of passengers booked, weight of the freight to be stowed in the cargo compartment, head winds, and weather at the plane's destination. Computers give much of this information, but it takes an alert mind to put the information together as she confers with the meteorologist and the crew of each flight regarding the best flight plan for its operation. The flight dispatcher must have a Federal Aviation Administration dispatcher's license and has moved up from jobs such as dispatch clerk, junior flight dispatcher, radio operator, meteorologist, or manager of a small station.

Schedule Coordinator

Next down the corridor is the schedule coordinator, an employee who must keep track of all aircraft and crews coming into or leaving the airport. If an airplane is delayed, he informs everyone concerned about the change. When an airplane has to be taken out of service, he must order a substitute which may mean checking out other flights or canceling another flight if no back-up plane is available.

Whenever an extra airplane is needed, he or she must first take into consideration what servicing or maintenance may be required and whether there is enough legal flight time left for the aircraft to fly before its next regular maintenance overhaul.

But there is more to the job. He handles crew scheduling and must learn who is sick, on vacation, or having a day off, as well as who has the most seniority. It is also impossible to schedule a pilot for a New York-Chicago run who has been authorized only to pilot on a New York-Houston run. The schedule coordinator must have had considerable experience in the operations office before he or she is assigned to this demanding post.

Meteorologist–Radio Operator

Glancing at our watch we realize our flight will be leaving soon which means we must hurry. We pass by the metorologist who assists in plotting flight plans. He has a college degree with a major in meteorology, may even have had experience with the United States Weather Bureau or a military weather service.

In another room loud speakers are blaring conversations between distant airplane crews and the radio operators sitting here before microphones. These operators are always on duty ready to maintain contact with all planes in order to give and receive messages as the aircraft proceed to their destinations. These operators have had special training in technical schools and obtained their radio operators' licenses from the Federal Communications Commission.

Food Service Jobs

At the end of the corridor, we peer through a glass door to see a huge kitchen where food is prepared for all departing flights on which meals will be served. Here are positions with titles such as pantry worker, dishwasher, salad maker, baker, steward chef, commissary chef, chief chef, supervisor, and assistant buyer. High school graduates who can obtain a health certificate will find this a good place to start their careers in food service because if they have interest and aptitude, they will be trained and advanced on the job.

Flight Attendants

With the smell of fresh baked Parker House rolls in our nostrils we run back upstairs to the departure lounge just in time to board our airplane. Two flight attendants greet us, show us to our seats, take our coats, and bring evening newspapers. They have been trained in the company's training school in a five-week intensive course in specific subjects such as routes, schedules, flight regulations, first aid, emergency procedures, good grooming, etiquette, and the proper serving of beverages and food. After graduation the first assignments are usually to fill in on extra flights or substitute for those on vacation or sick leave. Later, assignments are made on the basis of seniority so that experienced attendants have their choices of flights and times. Advancement is probably limited to becoming a flight service instructor in the training school, a passenger service representative, receptionist, or recruiting representative in the personnel department.

Flight Crew

Once our aircraft is airborne we are invited to visit the cockpit and meet the crew. The captain sits on the left hand seat in front of the instrument panel which displays a confusing array of gauges, dials, levers, and buttons. To the captain's right is the first officer. Behind, in a little recess, the walls of which resemble the instrument panel, is the ever-watchful flight engineer who constantly is alert for any signs of malfunctioning equipment and who also has certain duties which involve adjusting and operating various equipment.

New airline pilots usually start as flight engineers. Although airlines prefer an applicant who has a flight engineer's license, they may train a new employee who only has a commercial pilot's license.

"What are the requirements for becoming a pilot?" we asked the captain as he relaxed for a moment, the first officer having taken over the controls.

"You must be at least eighteen and a high school graduate, but most airlines require two years of college and prefer college graduates," he replied. "You must be able to pass a strict physical exam, have 20/20 vision with or without glasses, and have good hearing. You must pass a written test which includes questions on the principles of safe flight, navigation techniques, and FAA regulations. Of course, you must be able to demonstrate your flying ability to the FAA examiner."

The captain smiled and turned in his seat. "That's not all. Pilots who are going to fly in bad weather must be licensed by the FAA to fly by instruments. This calls for 40 hours of experience in instrument flying, passing a written examination, and demonstrating your ability in instrument flying." He paused to point at himself. "Those of us who are captains also have to obtain an airline transport pilot's license. To get this piece of paper, you have to be at least 23, have a minimum of 1500 hours of flying experience, and make certain that includes both night and instrument flying."

"Very interesting," we observed, "but where does one learn to fly?"

"I believe that the FAA has now certified some 1400 civilian flying schools, including a few colleges and universities which offer degree credit for pilot training. It's also possible to learn for nothing by joining one of the military services where you can gain considerable jet experience. I'd advise any young person interested in sitting up here in the cockpit to get a college education, then a pilot's license, and a flight engineer's license. This is one business in which you can't be over-qualified!"

A *List of Certified Pilot Schools* may be obtained by writing the US Department of Transportation, Publications Section, M-443.1, Washington, DC 20590.

Now we are back in the cabin, our seat belts are fastened. As the plane makes the final approach for landing we swoop down over the company's flight attendants training school and flight training academy near the airport. The flight instructors have had airline experience plus some teaching experience which qualifies them to teach new flight crew members and to check them periodically once they have started working.

"Please remain in your seats until the seat belt sign has been turned off," the stewardess requests. A few minutes later we are walking through the passenger terminal heading for the limousine to take us downtown where the company's headquarters offices are located.

AIRLINE MANAGEMENT

In contrast to the hubbub at the airport, the six floors of dignified offices high in a city skyscraper at first seem almost uninteresting, if not dull. This impression is wrong, though, for the more we learn about what goes on within these walls, which are so remote from the airplanes, the more fascinating it all becomes.

The Reservations Department

Our first stop is in the reservations department. Here, all of the incoming telephone calls requesting information or reservations are received by numerous reservations agents, each of whom works within a tiny cubicle. Apart from the headset, a copy of the company's schedules and tariffs, and the *Official Airline Guide,* which contains schedules of all the airlines, the only other equipment is the computer terminal. This is connected to the reservations computer center which is located in another city 600 miles away.

The computer is really an electronic brain with a fantastic memory. When a passenger requests a seat on a certain flight, the agent asks the computer if there is space on that particular trip and to the destination requested by the customer. The answer is flashed back instantly. Then the agent is able to make the reservation by typing the date, flight number, destination, and the passenger's name, address, and telephone number. This information is stored in the computer. Later it will be retrieved when it is time to see how many passengers are booked for that flight and a passenger manifest is prepared.

The reservations department or the ticket counter are two of the best places to start one's airline career. Usually a week or ten days' classroom instruction in routings and fares is followed by three weeks of on-the-job training. At this time, the agent is considered ready to work independently. The knowledge and experience gained in these positions give one an invaluable background for future advancement.

Sales Positions

The reservations department is part of the general sales department which is located on the floor above. Although airlines depend for the most part on their newspaper, magazine, radio, and TV advertising as well as on the thousands of travel agents for their customers, a number of specialists are needed to handle various sales functions.

Walking through the corridors we are able to get a good idea of the range of sales activities by looking at the names of the different divisions which we pass:

- *Passenger Sales Division.*   Responsible for planning and carrying out sales programs.
- *Freight Sales Division.*   Same as above, but for freight.
- *Reservations and Ticket Offices Division.*   Oversees the operation of all reservations and ticket offices, planning and opening new offices, and training new employees.
- *Interline Sales Division.*   Encourages other airlines to route as much business as possible on each other's planes.
- *Agency Sales Division.*   Plans programs designed to increase the cooperation of travel agencies in booking business with the airline.
- *Convention Sales Division.*   Contacts organizations which will be holding large conventions and persuades convention delegates to use the airline.
- *Tariff Division.*   Computes and publishes all of the company's fares and freight tariffs.
- *Schedule Division.*   Prepares and publishes all the schedules for both the passenger planes and airfreighters which the company will operate.
- *Advertising Division.*   Prepares and places all company advertising.

In talking with one of the sales executives we ask how one prepares for a position in the sales department.

"Many of our people have transferred from the reservations and ticket offices division," he said. "On the other hand, we hire college graduates who have backgrounds in transportation, economics, statistics, business administration, or computer operation, and find that they learn quickly and become very satisfactory employees."

Public Relations and Purchasing

Taking the elevator to the next floor as we continue our tour of the headquarters building, we come to the public relations department. Its mission is to provide the public with information about the company, at the same time promoting that company's image. Whenever an airline has a problem newsworthy enough to make the TV newscast or headlines, it is the job of the public relations department to see to it that it receives sympathetic treatment.

"All of our staff is devoted to just one purpose," the public relations director told us, "and that is telling the outside world about our airline and how great it is. But when we have a serious accident, we pull hard on the reversing lever and all our efforts are bent on toning down the news reports and trying to see that the TV, radio, and newspapers are factual in their reporting and free of sensationalism."

To our query regarding job opportunities in his department the executive replied: "Apart from the clerical positions we like to hire men and women from schools which specialize in public relations or journalism. Sometimes we take a man or woman who has a newspaper background."

The much larger purchasing department is across the hall. Here we learn that millions of dollars are spent annually by staff members as they buy everything from paper clips to multimillion dollar airplanes. Most of the buying is done by purchasing agents or buyers with new employees being assigned to work with a senior member of the department. College degrees are necessary for good positions and beginning jobs require that you at least have an associate degree program in purchasing.

THE FINANCE DEPARTMENT

Occupying an entire floor, the sprawling finance department somehow reminds us of a bank. Its large area is filled with rows of desks at which men and women are working industriously. Here auditors, statisticians, financial analysts, economists, clerks, section and department heads are busy trying to keep track of the $1.5 million which flow in and out of the office each day from the innumerable ticket offices and freight depots.

The two most important sections of any airline finance department are revenue accounting, which keeps track of all incoming money, and disbursements, which pays all the bills. Closely associated with disbursements is the payroll section, responsible for preparing thousands of weekly and bi-weekly pay checks. We pause at the next section to chat briefly with the manager of the insurance section. His staff is concerned with handling every type of insurance from the multimillion dollar coverage on the aircraft fleet and passengers to the group life or health insurance which is available to all employees.

Moving along the aisle we find a group of employees who are familiar with both accounting procedures and tax laws. They staff the tax section, which houses an increasingly important group of specialists, because federal income taxes alone can run into the millions. Other taxes are collected by cities, counties, and states where the company's planes touch down.

The budget section crammed into one corner of the floor is most influential because these employees forecast income and expenses for the years ahead. They also review every departmental budget to make certain it is not too large in proportion to company assets.

Every section has its typists, secretaries, and accounting clerks, often called bookkeeping clerks, who have taken accounting or bookkeeping courses in school. They perform a wide variety of duties, mostly of a routine nature. The other more specialized positions call for men and women who have had college courses in economics, statistics, mathematics, or business administration. Those employees who have taken graduate work or attended a business school qualify for the more responsible posts, many of which lead to top management positions.

OTHER HOME OFFICE DEPARTMENTS

It has been a long day and now we conclude our tour by walking quickly through the remaining departments before everyone leaves at five o'clock.

Airlines own little or no property. They lease their office space and rent hangars as well as all of the lobbies, concourses, ticket counter areas and offices at airport terminals. Planning and supervising construction of hangars, ticket counters, office and other space, negotiating leases, and working closely with airport managements are the responsibilities of the properties department.

In the personnel department we see men and women busy interviewing and hiring applicants for jobs, keeping all of the personnel records, setting wage and salary scales, negotiating contracts with labor unions, and handling employee benefits.

Finally, after we pass the legal department, we stop at the door to the mail room. Here a number of young men and women are busy sorting and stamping mail, wrapping packages, and packing mail sacks for delivery to the post office. This is an ideal place for those just out of high school to start. Many an airline executive began his career sorting and delivering mail.

With a farewell wave to the receptionist we step into an elevator and go quickly to the ground floor. We have had an interesting day observing the operations of an airline which offers the greatest variety of career opportunities in the transportation industry.

FINDING YOUR JOB

If you live in a city served by several airlines, watch the help wanted newspaper advertisements and also apply at the personnel offices of those companies which offer the best opportunities for immediate employment and advancement. Should you live where there is no airline service or where only one or two carriers offer limited schedules, you must try a different approach. Check with your state employment security office to see what airline job listings, if any, it might have. If nothing is available, be sure to ask the

The ramp service worker who fills the fuel tanks of large airplanes can enjoy the satisfaction of outdoor work that is important to the industry. (Photo: United Air Lines.)

interviewer for any suggestions. Bear in mind that these specialists keep up to date on employment trends.

Write the personnel department of those airlines where you think you would like to work. You can obtain the names and addresses of all airlines by consulting the *World Aviation Directory* published by the Ziff-Davis Publishing Company or by obtaining a list of airlines from the Air Transport Association of America.

If you know anyone who works for an airline or has a friend employed by one of the carriers, talk with him or her to obtain first hand information. If possible, secure the name of someone in the personnel department whom you might contact directly by mail or in person.

Further information about the air transport industry may be obtained by writing the US Department of Transportation, Washington, DC 20590; the Air Transport Association of America, 1709 New York avenue, NW, Washington, DC 20006; or one or more of the unions of airline workers (see Appendix A). A companion VGM Career Horizons book, *Opportunities in Airline Careers,* gives extensive information about the airlines and the careers they offer.

Overleaf: The size and complexity of the harbor facility at San Francisco indicates the importance of maritime shipping to the life of the city. (Photo: Air News Photos.)

CHAPTER 6

CAREERS FOR
WATER LOVERS

"I must down to the seas again, to the lonely sea and the sky,
And all I ask is a tall ship and a star to steer her by."

On Sunday, March 1, 1936, the *SS California* put into San Pedro, California, her departure set for 6:00 the next morning. That afternoon the crew, which was from New York, held a meeting and agreed to demand equal pay with that being given the seamen who were working on the West Coast. It would mean $5 a month more for the deck and engine department crew, or $62.50 a month, and a monthly increase of $10 for stewards, giving them a monthly salary of $50. Early Monday morning Joe Curran, the crew's spokesman, delivered the ultimatum to the captain. Company response was immediate. A replacement crew was quickly recruited to take the place of the seamen who would certainly walk off the ship when their demands were refused.

This time was different, though. The crew refused to leave the ship or cast anchor. For three days the vessel remained tied up, the crew performing all its usual duties except to uncoil the heavy ropes restraining the ship.

"Mutiny!" and "Striking Seamen Face Charges of Mutiny!" headlines read. Editors and readers fumed at the strikers and especially at "mutineer" Curran. The strike became such a serious issue nationally, that on the third day Frances Perkins, Secretary of Labor, called from Washington to speak with Curran personally.

"You'll have to sail that ship out of there," she told the tough leader.

"Not until the crew gets some recognition as human beings," was Curran's answer.

After more conversation Mrs. Perkins finally asked: "Well, Joe, what is it you want?"

By the time the conversation ended, Curran had promised to do his best to get the crew to sail the ship back to New York. For her part, the labor secretary promised to use her influence to make certain that none of the crew were "intimidated, coerced or persecuted" when they reached home port. As the ship made its way down the coast, the International Seamen's Union (ISU) and the shipowners negotiated a $5 monthly increase for sailors on the Atlantic and Gulf coasts. But the moment the *California* docked, her next sailing was canceled and the seamen were fired. In Washington the Secretary of Commerce wanted to bring mutiny charges against the crew but President Roosevelt backed Mrs. Perkins' promise and they were not molested.

Now the smoldering fires of revolt burst into flame. When the $5 increase was approved, the ISU officials failed to press for an even more important demand: that all hiring be done through the union hall and that the agreement provide overtime pay. Heading the revolt against "indignity and exploitation" was able-bodied seaman, Joe Curran.

Joe was born in New York City in 1906. His father died while he was a small lad and he was boarded with a family in New Jersey. After finishing sixth grade he took a series of jobs and in 1922, at 16, decided that he wanted to go to sea in a big ship. What he found below deck astonished him. In many ships the crews' quarters were filthy, rat-infested holes; food was often putrid, hours were excessively long, and the pay was minimal. Worse yet, for the privilege of working under these conditions, a person had to bribe those in charge of hiring seamen. Little wonder that sailors on all coasts were rebelling. Their union, the ISU, was doing little to help them and many members even accused their union officials of participating in some of the unethical and illegal hiring practices.

The rest of the story can be found in the history books and the

National Maritime Union's publication, *On a True Course, The Story of the National Maritime Union, AFL-CIO.* On May 3, 1937, the rank and file seamen held a mass rally in New York and founded the National Maritime Union of America. It had a strong democratic constitution which included a provision rooting out discrimination. With Joe Curran at its head, the new union encountered many difficulties, especially with communists. But eventually the organization expanded and built a splendid headquarters building in New York and modern halls in several other port cities. In addition, it enabled its membership to win good wages, working conditions, and generous pensions, health, and welfare benefits.

Becoming an ablebodied seaman in pursuit of a career at sea is a far different experience now than earlier this century. You too might find it a satisfying and rewarding life work.

MARITIME JOBS

Before seeing what it is like to be a seaman, let's touch briefly on the job outlook for the merchant marine, because it is not wide open to newcomers.

In 1980 approximately twenty-four thousand officer and non-officer seamen worked aboard United States oceangoing vessels. There were, however, about one and a half times the number of employed sailors as there are jobs on ships. Sailors employed but not working were on long vacations or away from their ships because of illness or other reasons. Over half of men and women were working aboard freighters; most of the rest were on tankers. A very small percentage was found on freighter-passenger ships.

During the 1980s employment in the merchant marine is expected to decline, although there will be some job openings to replace sailors who retire, die, or quit their jobs. Probably most of these vacancies will be filled by unemployed experienced seamen. Few inexperienced applicants are expected to find jobs.

Employment is related to the number of ships in operation. During the early 1980s huge oil tankers were being taken out of service and cut apart for scrap because of the decline in the demand for oil.

At the same time some new ships were being constructed but they would be operated by smaller crews because so many of the tasks formerly assigned to seamen have been mechanized. For example, in the older, non-automated vessels, the engineering department carried twelve sailors, whereas there are only four in the newer ships.

This situation could change if the government were to require that a percentage of exported grains or imported oil must be carried in American ships. On the other hand, if the subsidies now paid to American shipowners by the government were reduced, employment would decline as the ships were withdrawn from service or switched to a foreign registry. One spark of hope is the possibility of new jobs in offshore oil and mineral exploration since sailors will be needed on oceanographic research and oil-exploration vessels.

MERCHANT MARINE UNLICENSED SAILORS

On a typical merchant ship, sailors make up most of the crew with each worker being assigned to one of the following departments: deck, engine, or steward's.

Deck Department

The entry rating (or grade) in the deck department is that of ordinary seaman who scrubs desks, coils and splices ropes, paints, cleans living quarters, and does other maintenance jobs. He may also relieve an able seaman and steer the ship or act as a lookout to watch for other ships.

Able seamen (often referred to as AB) have a thorough knowledge of every part of the ship and can handle all the gear and deck equipment. Sometimes they act as quartermasters, steer, and serve as lookout. Some of the skills expected of the able seaman include being able to tie common knots, handle mooring lines when the boat is docking or leaving, participate in boat drills, and be familiar with launching lifeboats and liferafts. They must also be familiar with fire prevention and control, and do general maintenance work such as is done by ordinary seamen.

The *boatswain* or *bosun* is the highest ranking able seaman. He supervises the deck crew, passes on orders from the deck officers, and makes certain that these orders are carried out. He assists the chief mate, directs the maintenance work, and when the ship docks he supervises the deck crew.

Engine Department

The entry position here is that of wiper. There are usually from one to three wipers on cargo ships who keep the engine room and machinery clean. Oilers lubricate equipment and may help overhaul and repair machinery; while firers-watertenders check and regulate the amount of water in the boilers, regulate the fuel flow, and check the operation of condensers and evaporators which convert salt to fresh water. The electrician repairs and maintains all electrical equipment and there may also be a refrigeration engineer to make certain all of the refrigerating equipment for perishable cargoes is operating properly.

Steward's Department

The preparation and serving of meals as well as the cleaning and maintenance of living quarters are the responsibilities of this department. Beginning jobs of utility hands and mess attendants require no skills. *Utility hands* bring food supplies from storerooms and refrigerators to the kitchen, prepare vegetables, wash cooking utensils, and scour the galley equipment. *Mess attendants* are responsible for setting tables, serving meals, washing the dishes, and cleaning the living quarters. The *chief cook, assistants,* and the *chief steward* must have cooking skills. With the increased use of frozen and prepackaged foods, and smaller crews, many ships need fewer personnel in this department.

Working Conditions

Working on a ship can subject you to great temperature extremes. Standing on the deck in the hot sun or during bitter cold windy weather for long periods of time as a lookout can be as uncomfortable as working in the engine room with its constant high temperature.

Accommodations for sailors are not luxurious, but good meals are served in a mess room which may double as a recreation hall. On older ships, crews share quarters and have little privacy, but new vessels have single berth rooms. However, even with improved conditions, work on a ship can become boring.

Sailors in the merchant marine work seven days a week although individuals usually work two four-hour watches or shifts during each 24-hour period, and have eight hours off between each watch. Some sailors are day workers who are on duty eight hours a day from Monday through Friday. When working over 40 hours a week, overtime is paid, and when the ship is in port, the basic workweek is 40 hours for all crew members.

Job Training

Although not required, a useful background for entering the merchant marine would be previous experience at sea in the Coast Guard or Navy.

A few high schools offer training for marine transportation careers. Perhaps the two outstanding are the Randal Aerospace and Marine Sciences High School in Washington, DC, and the Food and Maritime Trades High School in New York City which is located on two World War II ships. Several degree-granting as well as community colleges offer courses. (See *Lovejoy's College Guide* or one of the other guides for available college preparatory courses.) The Harry Lundeberg School, St. Mary's County, Piney Point, Maryland, is perhaps one of the best known professional schools which gives training in entry or beginning job skills as well as advanced courses. Those interested in becoming cooks should obtain information from the Marine Cooks and Stewards Training Program, 350 Fremont Street, San Francisco, CA 94105. The Seamen's Church Institute of New York, 15 State Street, New York, NY 10004, offers a variety of programs in the maritime field.

You can achieve advancement in the deck and engine departments by serving for certain periods of time in a particular job and then successfully passing a Coast Guard examination that tests ability to maintain and use equipment. Upgrading courses for sailors are offered by the two largest maritime unions, the National Maritime Union, and the Seafarers' International Union, as well as by some other organizations. In the steward's department, advancement is generally achieved by getting on-the-job training.

Basic Employment Procedures

According to a spokesperson for the National Maritime Union, there are few opportunities in today's mechant marine for the unskilled. It is no longer a job for people who just want to see the world or get away from it all. And he or she has to have more to offer than just physical strength and a desire to work. This is a brief description of how to get a job as unlicensed (non-officer) seaman in the US merchant marine:

> Every person employed aboard an ocean-going US ship must have a Seaman's Certificate which is issued by the United States Coast Guard. Before it will accept applications for a certificate, the Coast Guard requires that the applicant be referred by a recognized maritime training school or that he or she have a 'letter of commitment' from a shipping company or union addressed to the Coast Guard, stating there is a job available for her or him.
>
> *The NMU does not issue such letters of commitment. Most companies also do not issue them except in rare cases.* The flow of new seamen required to maintain the normal work force of the U.S. Merchant Marine is achieved mainly through the recruitment of people with certain needed skills or those who have come through maritime training schools or have had training in the armed forces in a skill needed in the merchant marine.
>
> After the Coast Guard issues you a Certificate, you register for shipping at the employment office of one of the seamen's unions or at a government agency that employs seamen. Also some oil companies and Harbor as well as Inland waterways companies do their own hiring. Without previous experience you would be in the lowest seniority group. Qualified seamen in higher senior-

ity groups usually have first claim on available jobs. In the NMU, within each seniority group, the person with the oldest registration card who has the qualifications has the option. A new person, therefore, would have to wait until a job comes down to the lowest seniority group and then must have the oldest card in that group. The job, when it comes, may be for a short trip, relieving the steady person on the job, and then the new seaman would be on the beach again. As he achieves higher seniority and higher skills, the waits are likely to become shorter and the jobs steadier.

There is no discrimination by race, creed, color or sex in NMU and no discrimination on grounds of membership or non-membership in the Union. Applicants can be barred for narcotic offenses or other criminal records and other specific evidence of unsuitability for work at sea. This would be decided jointly by the companies and the union, according to law.

Service in the armed forces is not by itself a factor in determining a new seaman's seniority rating. Service on foreign ships also does not count. Only seatime on American-flag merchant vessels is considered for seniority according to set rules. However, applicants with special skills which the merchant marine needs at the time would be given special consideration by a joint company-union panel.

The Service Fee at the National Maritime Union at this time is $52.50 and must be paid at the time of registration. You must have your U.S. Coast Guard Seaman's Certificate at the time you register. The Service Fee entitles the applicant to employment services through the Hiring Hall under the NMU National Shipping Rules for the regular shipping period of 90 days. *Registration carries no guarantee of employment and no refunds are made.* Regular dues in NMU are $60 per quarter (three months) and a seaman is obliged to apply for membership after serving 30 days on an NMU contract vessel. The initiation fee, after acceptance for membership, is $700.

The period of waiting for a job, once you are registered, depends on how many vessels come into port needing replacements in your category and how many seamen are on the beach waiting for that job. *You must be present in the hall in order to apply for any job.*

For further information about jobs for merchant marine sailors write the Office of Maritime Labor and Training, Maritime Administration, US Department of Transportation, 400 7th Street, Washington, DC 20590. Maritime unions can provide information also and if none are located near you, write to one of those which is listed in Appendix A.

MERCHANT MARINE OFFICERS

So far we have been describing employment opportunities for seamen who make up the largest group of workers aboard a ship. Those in charge of the vessel are the ship's officers, headed by the captain. He has complete responsibility and authority for operating the boat as well as for the safety of the passengers, crew, cargo, and the vessel itself. Serving beneath the captain are officers in the deck and engine departments, as well as a purser who is a staff officer. He handles all the required paper work including payrolls, and assists passengers as needed. Some pursers have been trained also as physician's assistants.

To qualify as an officer you must be at least 21, be a United States citizen, obtain a U.S. Public Health Service certificate attesting to your vision, color perception, and general physical condition, and have had at least three years of appropriate sea experience or have graduated from an approved training program. To advance to higher ratings, officers must pass progressively more difficult examinations.

Your best means of becoming a well-trained officer is to attend one of the established training programs such as are available at the US Merchant Marine Academy at Kings Point, New York 11024 which admits students on the same basis as the military academies. You may also want to investigate one or more of the six state maritime academies: California Maritime Academy, Vallejo, CA 94591; Great Lakes Maritime Academy, Traverse City, MI 49684; Maine Maritime Academy, Castine, ME 04421; Massachusetts Maritime Academy, Buzzards Bay, MA 02532; Texas Maritime College, Galveston, TX 77553; and State University of New York Maritime College, Fort Schuyler, Bronx, N.Y. 10465. Except for the Great

Lakes Maritime Academy which is discussed in a later section, all of these institutions are four-year colleges.

A number of trade unions in the maritime industry also provide officer training. It should be noted that beginning in 1986 graduates of the US Merchant Maritime Academy must serve at least five years in the merchant marine or the military.

The working hours for officers on board ship are similar to those for seamen. Most officers belong to a maritime union, and enjoy excellent pay and living conditions aboard ship.

PORTSIDE JOBS

The merchant marine could not operate without the men and women responsible for loading and unloading the ships at portside, and those who work in offices doing the necessary planning, record-keeping, accounting, and purchasing.

In the old days stevedores or longshoremen performed all of the manual labor of carrying cargo on and off vessels, but much of that work is now performed by lift trucks and cranes, which cut down the need for manual workers. The introduction of containerization has reduced the employment of longshoremen too, but there are still opportunities for these workers as the following job titles suggest:

Carloaders load and unload railroad cars, trucks, containers, and barges. Ship cleaners clean the ship's hold, wash painted surfaces, clean and check lifeboats and living quarters, and perform other duties. Marine carpenters crate and pack cargo, repair pallets, and do other work related to wood. Timekeepers keep track of work performed on the docks, ships, barges, and terminals. Billing and manifest clerks do the paper work while checkers keep track of all goods received or shipped. In addition there is the usual cadre of guards, watchmen, mechanics, crane operators, ship maintenance personnel, truck drivers, and other workers.

Most ports have an organization called a Port Authority which controls activities of the harbor. Many of them have training programs and may be helpful in giving advice about employment. You can obtain a list of such authorities from the American Association of Port Authorities, 1612 K Street, NW, Washington, DC 20006.

Although many harbor workers learn on the job, clerical and technical skills can be learned in high school or a vocational school. A college degree or previous experience as a ship's officer is helpful when applying for the administrative jobs.

One other area in the portside is the familiar tug boat which in some harbors is essential for pulling the larger ships into and out of the harbor as well as for towing barges. Here is an opportunity to work on a ship without ever going to sea. (See the next section which discusses tug boats.)

INLAND MARITIME CAREERS

Few Americans are aware of the extensive inland waterway system which includes the Great Lakes, the intercoastal system, and rivers such as the "Mighty Mississippi." Actually about 15 percent of America's total transportation now moves on its inland waters.

Barges carry much of this freight, which consists principally of chemicals, grains, forest products, iron, steel, and petroleum products. These vessels are not manned nor are they self-propelled, but are pulled by a tug or pushed by a towboat.

Here is a world apart from that of the merchant marine. Instead of three departments, each with its set of specialists, most towboats have a crew of two, the captain or master, and the pilot or mate. They work together closely, each standing two six hour watches daily. If it is a longer route there may be a second mate and they stand two four hour watches per day the same as seamen. Those boats which ply the western rivers or the Gulf of Mexico inland waterways need a steersman who steers the vessel while an engineer is on duty down in the hold in the engine room if it is a larger boat. Towboat cooks are responsible for serving the food they prepare, but deckhands may perform this work on smaller boats.

Responsibilities of the deckhand vary according to the size of the boat and its cargo. Aside from routine duties on the boat, the deckhand ties together the barges to be pulled and later breaks them apart when they reach their port of destination. He usually works six hours on, six off, a certain number of days on and off each month, creating a type of schedule and life-style which will not appeal to everyone. The work can be dangerous and boring too, but the chance to travel over the waterways has a definite appeal to many.

Another important position is that of the tankerman who loads and unloads liquid cargoes. En route he watches the condition of the liquid, checks pumps and engines. He may also work in ports refueling seagoing vessels from bunker barges.

Employment Opportunities

Again, in contrast to the merchant marine, this part of the industry is expected to continue its expansion and therefore will need skilled personnel. It has been estimated that the approximate eighty thousand men and women working on barges and inland boats will increase by 350 to 500 percent over the next fifty years. As the barges and other vessels become more complex, those interested in working on them will need more specific skills too.

The Great Lakes Shipping Industry

Here is one career you may want to explore: ship's officer aboard a ship which serves ports on the great Lakes. The lake fleet and their personnel are part of the U.S. Merchant Marine and the need for highly trained men and women to operate these ships is growing thanks to the impending retirement of many officers and the increase in guaranteed time off such officers enjoy.

The Great Lakes Maritime Academy specializes in training merchant marine officers for Great Lakes vessels. Affiliated with Northwestern Michigan College, this three-year maritime program awards an Associate of Applied Science Degree and qualifies all successful cadets to take the U.S. Coast Guard examination for a First Class Pilot's License (Great Lakes), or Third Assistant Engineer's License (steam and motor vessels).

A new class begins each summer, and to be eligible for admission you must meet the following basic requirements: be a US citizen 17 years of age or older; meet all US Coast Guard requirements; possess a high school diploma or equivalent with an academic grade point average of 2.0 (C) or better; successfully complete at least one year of high school level courses in algebra, physics and/or chemistry; complete the American College Test or equivalent college entrance examination and achieve the following scores: combined ACT English, mathematics, and composite standard scores: 50; minimum ACT English standard score: 15; and minimum ACT mathematics standard score: 16.

Deadline for completing applications for the annual June entering class is January 31. For further details write: Admissions Officer, Great Lakes Maritime Academy, Traverse City, MI 49684.

Great Lakes Sailors' Job Referral Centers are located at 2132 West 25th Street, Cleveland, OH 44113; 602 Dearborn Drive, Toledo, OH 43605; 3501 East 106th Street, Chicago, IL 60617; and 730 East Superior Street, Duluth, MN 55802.

OTHER MARINE CAREERS

You do not have to join the merchant marine to find a career in water transportation. Opportunities may lie close to your home if you live on or near the shore. Consider some of the following.

Operation of all day fishing boats for fishermen who enjoy the sport of deep-sea fishing is a growing business. Boats usually leave early in the morning and return sometime during the late afternoon. Typical advertisements read: "Captain Jones will leave the West Dock daily at 6:00 A.M. for deep-sea fishing ten miles out." Ask the captain of each boat about possible job opportunities. Here you may find good summer or part-time jobs which will give you valuable experience.

In some areas commercial fishing boats depart for distant fishing grounds and remain at sea for several days or weeks as they fill their holds with valuable catches. Even a short-term job on one of these boats can provide experience.

The growth and popularity of private boating has created an expanding marina business. A busy marina is an interesting place to work. Although you may not do much traveling, you will learn how to handle boats, and occasionally have a chance to get out on the

A crew member on a tug boat will spend nearly all of a working life on the water.

water. In the north, marinas are a summer business and therefore only offer temporary jobs.

In many parts of the country excursion boats take passengers to distant points of interest or just tour a harbor. They provide jobs for deckhands, engineers, and others in the maritime field, as do ferries.

Pick up a Sunday newspaper from a large city and turn to the travel section. You cannot help but be impressed by the number of advertisements for cruises. The era of luxurious trans-Atlantic or trans-Pacific ocean voyages is practically gone, except for the occasional trip, but in their place are luxurious cruises which range all the way from three-day trips to around-the-world voyages. If you study these advertisements you will note that they may reveal that the ships are of foreign registry. This means that they do not have to observe the stringent American rules which apply to the operation of passenger liners. Furthermore, if they are owned and operated by foreign companies, they are usually staffed by natives of their countries. This may not be true of all the ships which call at a port near you, and certainly not of excursion boats which offer simple daytime or overnight trips. Since cruise ships are, in reality, floating hotels with every conceivable service for passengers, the list of job opportunities could be long. Your state employment security office may be able to tell you about openings with the cruise lines, and you should also apply directly to the cruise line offices.

Further information about the maritime industry may be obtained by writing the Office of Maritime Labor and Training, Maritime Administration, US Department of Transportation, Washington, DC 20590. A companion VGM Career Horizons book, *Opportunities in Marine and Maritime Careers,* will give you much more detailed information on the subject.

Overleaf: Patricia Friend, above, in front of her Kentworth (K-W) 400 Cummings 10-speed motor, has been a trucker for five years. Below, route controllers use computers and maps to keep track of shipments. (Photos: Patricia Friend and North American Van Lines.)

CHAPTER 7

CAREERS IN THE TRUCKING INDUSTRY

As late as the 1950s huge train yards were busy places in the afternoon. Noisy switch engines put the long freights together so that they would be ready for their scheduled departures in the evening. Some of the faster trains received imaginative names like Red Ball Express, Overland Limited, Merchants Dispatch, or Evening Mercury. Tower workers, conductors, engineers, and dispatchers paid more attention to running these trains on schedule than they did to unprofitable passenger trains. Nevertheless, the future was not bright for the rails. The nation's 40,000 mile interstate highway system had been creeping over mountains, through valleys, and over rivers as it laid mile after mile of smooth four-lane roads which opened exciting new prospects for truckers both large and small.

What happened to the New York, New Haven & Hartford Railroad in New England was typical. Before the New England Thruway (Interstate 95) opened in the late 1950s, numerous fast freights snaked their way along the heavily traveled New York-Boston Atlantic coastline route. Then with the opening of Interstate Highway 95, which enabled trucks to roar between these two cities in four hours, more and more freight was diverted from freight cars to trailer trucks. Lower rates and better service enticed more and more shippers to try the trucks.

Except for heavy shipments of bulk materials such as grain, coal, oil, lumber, livestock, chemicals, and liquified gas, the railroads were forced to relinquish most of their business to the trucks. Eventually short haul railroads like the New Haven went into bankruptcy. They then lost their identities altogether as they were forced to merge with other carriers in order to survive.

There are two kinds of truck freight: *Less Than Truckload* or *LTL,* and *Truckload.* Less than truck-load means cargo consisting of a quantity of items which are insufficient to fill a large truck.

Companies which provide LTL service have smaller trucks which make several stops to pick up enough freight to fill a larger tractor-trailer truck. This truck then carries its cargo to a control terminal where the packages are sorted and other trucks haul the packages to terminals in various cities. There, they are sorted again and put on smaller trucks for door-to-door delivery.

The second category of freight, *truckload,* refers to a truck which picks up a complete load of goods from one shipper and hauls it directly to a single company or location in another city. Most of the new companies entering the trucking industry are interested in the truckload business because it is less expensive to operate and may be run with non-union labor.

Make no mistake; trucking is a huge business. It is one of the most important in the transportation field, taking in approximately $50 billion annually. During a recent year, long-distance motor trucks hauling intercity freight ranked second to the railroads. The trains carried 36 percent of all freight. Motor trucks carried 25 percent.

Back in 1930, Galen Rousch, an attorney, and his brother Carroll founded a small company in Akron, Ohio, which they called Roadway Express. Today the company's headquarters are still in Akron and it has become the number one trucker. It grew by buying up smaller companies and then extending its routes throughout the country. With approximately 25,000 tractors, trailers, and trucks, and as many employees, the company takes in over a billion dollars in revenue annually. In a recent year it accepted over 12 million shipments which it handled in its terminals in more than 400 cities.

The number one career in trucking is that of driver. Since it offers one of the more glamorous and better paying jobs, and does not require specialized formal education, let's first of all look at what is required to be a long-distance truck driver.

Earnings of each driver will vary, though, depending on the number of miles he or she drives, the number of hours worked, and the type of truck driven.

In addition to the vehicles operated by the large, long-distance companies there are firms such as dairies and bakeries which own their own fleets and pay their drivers on the same basis as their other employees. Usually the wage is for a specified number of hours and if the drivers work additional hours, they are paid overtime. A workweek of at least fifty hours is not uncommon. These drivers sometimes belong to the unions which represent the other plant employees, whereas most men and women who are long-distance drivers are members of the International Brotherhood of Teamsters.

Qualifications and Training

Minimum qualifications for long-distance truck drivers who are engaged in interstate commerce are set by the Department of Transportation. You must be at least 21 years old, pass a physical examination, have good hearing, 20/40 vision with or without glasses, the normal use of arms and legs, and normal blood pressure.

Some trucking companies have additional hiring standards. Many have a minimum age of twenty-five, others specify height and weight limitations. Some require applicants to have had several years experience driving trucks long distances. All employers seek men and women with good driving records who can pass a road test operating the type of truck which will be driven in regular service. In addition, they must take a written examination on the Motor Carrier Safety Regulations of the US Department of Transportation and in most states truck drivers must have a chauffeur's license, or commercial driving permit.

A high school driver-training course is good background and a high school course in automotive mechanics is also helpful inasmuch as it will enable you to make minor roadside repairs. Some technical-vocational schools offer truckdriving courses. But before taking such a course, check with prospective employers to make certain that the school's training is acceptable. A more common method of entering a truckdriving career is to start as a dockworker and advance from this position to driving a small panel truck and then perhaps a larger truck in local service.

Newly–hired drivers are taught how to prepare the forms used on the job, receive a small amount of driving instruction and practice on a training course to learn how to maneuver the larger trucks. Then they will make one or more training trips under the supervision of an instructor or experienced driver.

Opportunities for promotion are limited, generally only to positions as safety supervisor, driver supervisor, or dispatcher. Most drivers are not interested in these jobs, however, because the starting pay usually is less than they earn in driving positions.

For further information about career opportunities in long-distance trucking write the American Trucking Association, Inc., 1616 P Street, NW, Washington, DC 20036.

LOCAL TRUCK DRIVERS

Local trucks, which operate within a city, town, or limited area, usually do the initial pickups from plants and factories, and take freight to terminals where it may be consolidated with other shipments or placed directly on a long-distance truck. These same local trucks may pick up freight which has arrived at the terminal and then deliver it to stores and homes.

Local truck drivers must be skilled and able to maneuver their vehicles through dense traffic and into tight parking spaces, thread their way through narrow alleys, and expertly back up to loading platforms.

The trucking industry is so diversified that it is impossible to mention all the types of companies which offer career possibilities. If this business interests you, obtain a chauffeur's license and start your job search right at home by considering some of the businesses which operate their own trucks.

Some of these businesses employ drivers who are combination salespeople and drivers, as in many laundry, dry cleaning, milk, and bakery businesses. Don't overlook the possibilities of a career as a driver with a fuel oil supplier who sells gasoline, bottled gas, and heating oil. A lumber yard which makes deliveries of building supplies, a road construction company fleet of trucks and other heavy equipment, a bulk milk company which delivers milk in huge stainless steel containers, and the small retail stores which operate one or more delivery trucks and could offer employment opportunities.

OPPORTUNITIES FOR NON-DRIVERS

Not everyone wants to be a truck driver, nor can everyone qualify for the position. There are many other job opportunities in the trucking industry. We have already noted that Roadway Express employed upwards of 25,000 employees and the next largest company, Consolidated Freightways, had over 16,000 employees. These are but two of several large trucking firms, all of which need a variety of skills to operate their far-flung businesses successfully.

The truck on the road is like the tip of the iceberg. To keep the trucks filled and running every day calls for a huge, nationwide organization. The latest in management methods, computer technology, communication equipment, and automotive maintenance, keep the company going and the trucks moving.

Take Consolidated Freightways, for example. There, when a customer telephones an order for a shipment to be picked up, he sets in motion a highly efficient system. A trained employee takes down the details, and the minute the customer hangs up, the order is telephoned by radio to the nearest radio-controlled truck so that the driver can swing by the plant and make the pickup. As soon as the freight is loaded on the truck, the driver gives the customer a "pro" or identifying number. Later, if he should have any questions about the shipment, the information can be retrieved instantly from the computer by using this number.

While the truck is on its way to make the pickup, the pricing is being done by the computer. All the necessary paper work, such as writing up a bill of lading and preparing the manifest, are also being done electronically.

The location of the truck with the recent pickup, and the location of every other truck the company is operating, appear on a huge map of the United States in a control center. This system enables employees to monitor every vehicle continuously and pinpoint just where any shipment is in a matter of seconds. Thanks to long line telephone communications, all company operations are coordinated throughout the country.

As for customer relations, hundreds of representatives contact shippers and are available to help answer questions, solve problems, or assist in planning and shipping programs.

Imagine the fascination of working as a member of such a team in some clerical capacity as an accountant, or a computer, communications, or management specialist.

When surveying the trucking industry let's not forget those hundreds of truck terminals, airfreight depots, and special sales offices, each staffed with personnel who handle all the clerical functions, in addition to the dock personnel who load and unload the trucks and sort freight, as well as the mechanics and others who service and repair the vehicles. Here is an essential business which uses workers with many skills to keep freight moving twenty-four hours a day, seven days a week.

Although the large trucking companies move much of the nation's heavy freight, there is another nationwide company which specializes in transporting only small packages, none weighing more than fifty pounds. It is probably the best known trucker in the United States.

THE FLEET OF BROWN TRUCKS

Sitting behind a desk that had once been a lunch counter, the young man was busy answering the two old-fashioned telephones which rang from time to time. His new undertaking, the American Messenger Company, consisted of the phones, two bicycles, six messengers, and himself, James Casey. It was 1907 and his basement office was located in downtown Seattle.

The messengers had to be courteous and neat to impress Mr. Casey and qualify for a job. They delivered papers and articles for local businesses and individuals in the Seattle area. Occasionally they were called upon to walk dogs, and carry an elderly woman's groceries.

Business was not brisk but the tiny enterprise grew gradually. Casey changed the name to Merchants Parcel Delivery in 1913. At the same time he bought his first horseless carriage, a Model-T Ford. A year later seven motorcycles were added and soon Merchants was handling all the deliveries for three of the largest department stores in the Seattle area.

In 1919 the company opened an office in Oakland and changed its name to United Parcel service, at the same time adopting the official UPS color, brown. Other "firsts" followed such as the first brown uniforms for drivers, the first substation in Long Beach, and the first conveyor belt which was 180 feet long. It made handling packages more efficient.

The employee magazine, *The Big Idea,* appeared in Los Angeles in 1924. In its first issue Jim Casey wrote: "Here's to the success of the *Big Idea,* as a means of fostering a spirit of friendship, cooperation, and good will among all of us who are brought together by UPS. The business has grown to the size where it it no longer possible for all of us to know each other so intimately as would naturally be the case. But, it is intended that this shall always be a human organization. I want all to know some of the purposes, policies, and ideas of this company to the end that the greater possible good may come to customers and employees alike." Today each UPS District has its own local *Big Idea* which includes twelve to sixteen pages of companywide news.

It seemed that nothing could stop the growth of this dynamic company. UPS service was extended to every major West Coast city. Then the first brown trucks started rolling on New York City streets on July 14, 1930, and by year end the fleet was delivering all parcels for 123 stores. Soon people in midwestern states were seeing the brown trucks and today every state except Alaska is served by the company.

In 1953 the management decided to offer UPS service not only to businesses but to anyone who wants to ship a parcel. By the 1980s UPS was employing over ninety thousand men and women, operating some forty thousand delivery and feeder vehicles, and maintaining hundreds of buildings spread across the nation. These buildings house highly specialized sorting devices.

The secret of UPS's success is consolidating packages at every point from pickup to delivery. This system enables the company to deliver the maximum number of packages in a minimum amount of time and miles. The small package shipments of some 300,000 shippers are fed into one highly specialized system. That system starts in the package car as the driver delivers packages and at the same time picks up those articles ready for shipment.

All these packages are then consolidated at the nearest center with those picked up by other drivers. Tractor trailer units feed the packages from surrounding centers into a hub facility each night. Here they are all sorted and loaded into outgoing feeder vehicles which will take them to the UPS facility closest to their destination. Thanks to a highly mechanized sorting system a hub like that at Montgomery, Alabama, can handle about 34,000 packages each night in less than four hours.

An equal amount of attention is given to the loading of each delivery truck. By the time each driver arrives for work he or she finds that other workers have loaded the truck in the proper sequence so that deliveries can be made as quickly as possible over the most direct route.

No matter how remote the address of either the shipper or receiver, UPS pickup and delivery service is available and each package is delivered directly to the door of the consignee. In addition, the company maintains customer counters at each of the operating locations. Here individuals and business shippers can bring their packages rather than have them picked up.

As you may well imagine, this nationwide service depends on people: the men or women who answer the telephones and take your orders for pickups; the drivers who deliver and pick up the packages; the sorters at the various facilities; the drivers of the huge tractors and trailers which carry the packages long distances between centers and hubs; the maintenance people who keep the trucks clean and in top operating condition; the various clerical people in the offices; and the supervisory and administrative staff—all help keep UPS going.

UPS is an efficient company which standardizes and codes all of its operations. If you have a flat tire, you have a *471*; if you need road service, you call for a *388*. Neatness is still high on the list of personnel "musts." Trucks, too, must be clean and to keep them that way, they are washed every night.

Jim Casey, honorary chairman of the company, was ninety-two years old in 1980. He doubtless was pleased to see how his original fleet of one Model T and seven motorcycles had grown to 40,000 brown vehicles. The company's head office had moved from Seattle to the New York suburb of Greenwich, Connecticut. For further information about a career with this company write United Parcel Service, 51 Weaver Street, Greenwich, CT 06830.

THE LOCAL AND LONG DISTANCE MOVERS

Another large segment of the trucking industry is devoted to moving. These companies transport furniture, pianos, and other household goods.

Back in 1891 two brothers living in Sioux City, Iowa, decided to earn their fame and fortune. They obtained a large cart, a strong horse, and lettered the side of the wagon: "Bekins, Moving & Storage." John and Martin Bekins had very little money, but lots of ambition and a sincere interest in each customer's individual needs.

Ninety years later Bekins had grown to become the largest moving and storage company in the world with over 400 locations in the United States and operations in more than 100 foreign countries. The company claimed that the brothers' original spirit was sustained and that personal service was still the cornerstone of the business even though the company handles more than 900 moves each day.

This may seem like an astronomical number of moves for just one company, but perhaps it is not so surprising when you consider that about 40 million Americans, or a fifth of the population, move each year. It is the moving and storage industry which makes it possible for families to pack up and make moves of hundreds or thousands of miles, with every detail surrounding the move anticipated and handled efficiently.

Furniture movers employed by interstate companies often work in crews of three or four, one of whom is the driver who also loads and unloads along with the other movers. If one of the helpers is qualified to drive the truck, it may be possible for the van to make an uninterrupted long-distance trip. Such movers may be away from home for weeks at a time. They lead irregular lives with sixty hours of work being considered a normal work week.

Ability to read, write, and do arithmetic, a strong back, good coordination, a sense of responsibility, and a willingness to be helpful and courteous are the main personal requirements for this job. Drivers must hold a Class 1 driver's license for the kind of equipment they will be driving. Many companies give their employees training in both packing and driving.

The majority of furniture movers work for local companies which do short haul or local moving and also act as agents for interstate and international movers. The large moving companies have their own movers who may travel throughout the country as they transport several loads before returning to their regular terminal.

As the population continues to grow and people keep changing homes, the demand for movers should increase somewhat. Promotion is possible for a mover to the position of estimator. This person determines the weight and cost of shipping a houseful of furniture. A mover with a thorough knowledge of the business might be considered for promotion to dispatcher. The dispatcher is responsible for routing all the trucks and keeping in touch with all the drivers.

In addition to the usual clerical positions, there are openings for billing clerks, claims adjusters, maintenance workers, mechanics, and administrative personnel.

A word of warning: the moving business is a seasonal one. The busiest time is during the summer months of June, July, August, and September when children are not in school. The last week of each month is usually the busiest time.

For the names and addresses of prospective employers, look in the yellow pages of your telephone book under Movers. For further information write American Trucking Association, Inc., 1616 P Street, NW, Washington, DC 20036.

Because trucking is vital to American industry, a career in this sector of transportation is well worth considering. Although much of America's freight moves long-distance by air and rail, remember that in most instances the shipments must reach the plane or freight car by truck. At their destination they must be trucked again.

Overleaf: This new $15-million computerized freight classification yard in Sheffield, Alabama, helps railroad officials keep track of their cargo. (Photo: Southern Railway System.)

CHAPTER 8

NEW HORIZONS
FOR RAIL CAREERS

"Imagine this if you will.

You're speeding to Washington on the all-new Metroliner Express Service. Your scheduled running time: a remarkable 2 hours and 59 civilized minutes.

Your body is relaxing in a big, wide, comfortable reclining seat. The new, roomier 60-seat car creates an incredible amount of space all around you.

You pull up your leg rest, settle back, do some work, read. Later, you decide to stroll to the Lounge Car and you select from a menu that is better than ever. Hot meals. Cold snacks. Wine. Beer. Cocktails.

Or imagine that you opted for our new club car service.

Now you're enjoying a complimentary Continental breakfast. Or a light meal for lunch or dinner.

Or perhaps you wish to order from the menu. Here you peruse a variety of entrees, and you are served at your seat.

While you're dining you realize that you are now experiencing all the luxuries the Washington business traveler has long since given up.

But it's all happening now—speed and comfort—on Amtrak. Downtown to downtown. From Penn Station four times a day, every business day. To Washington. And back. (Plus there's also all-new service on our six other Metroliner trains every business day.)"

AMTRAK'S NEW METROLINER EXPRESS SERVICE

The above advertisement which appeared in the *New York Times* is indicative of the new look which Amtrak is assuming. The "prophets of doom" who say that railroading is obsolete should ride one of these fine trains or some of the other Amtrack limiteds, or watch one of the Conrail freights speed by. They will agree that railroads are not only here to stay, but have an exciting future.

Unfortunately America's total rail mileage has shrunk considerably over the past fifty years as many unprofitable branches and even main lines were abandoned. As railroad companies merged or went out of business, most of the once luxurious passenger services disappeared. Commuting service continued to serve the suburbs thanks to state governments which started providing subsidies for these trains.

To understand the railroad picture, let's take a look at the two government-sponsored railroad corporations: Amtrak and Conrail.

AMTRAK AND CONRAIL

Amtrak

By 1970 more than 100 of the nation's 500 passenger railroads had asked the Interstate Commerce Commission for permission to discontinue all service. Since 1950 most of these privately owned companies had been operating their trains at a loss and were facing bankruptcy. The automobile, which could now speed over the new interstate highway system as well as other improved roads, provided a less expensive and more flexible form of transportation for many families which formerly traveled by train. At the same time the growth of airline service and the speed of the jets, which could fly coast-to-coast in less than six hours, contrasted with the three-day train trip, made transcontinental rail service practically obsolete. True, some people still preferred to ride trains or were afraid to fly but there were not enough of them.

In October 1970 Congress established Amtrak, officially known as the National Railroad Passenger Corporation. This was a quasi-public corporation, its board of directors composed of eight officers appointed by the president, three representatives from the railroad industry, and four private investors. These investors were chosen from those who held the company's preferred stock.

Congress intended the company to be a profit-making enterprise and gave it an initial grant of $40 million plus $100 million in federal loan guarantees. By the time Amtrak began operating in 1971, it had eliminated half of the intercity passenger service, keeping only those trains which enjoyed dense traffic. During that first year trains were running over 180 routes and serving approximately 300 cities.

Since that time Amtrak experienced many troubled years, but by 1982 the future looked bright. Not only had Amtrak boosted its on-time performance to 80 percent from 51 percent in 1978, but it had 284 new two-level Superliners to attract more traffic for the long-distance runs in the West. An important labor agreement covering most of its 18,000 workers was expected to save the company $132 million during the thirty-nine-month life of the contract.

Most exciting, however, were plans for a high speed Los Angeles-San Diego, 130-mile run, using Japanese bullet-train technology. If built, it is contemplated that about 100 trains a day, cruising at 160 miles an hour, would make the trip in fifty-nine minutes. Studies showed that as many as 12 million passengers might use the service. Other routes were also being studied for Florida, Texas, and Illinois.

Rail travel is swift, clean, energy efficient, and generally provides convenient service to downtown locations in the cities it serves. Since the first passenger train operated on the Baltimore and Ohio in 1830, nothing has appeared to improve on this ground transportation.

Conrail

Following the bankruptcy of the Penn-Central Railroad, the largest business failure in American history, Congress created the Consolidated Rail Corp., otherwise known as Conrail. The legislation became effective on April 1, 1976. From the ruins of six bankrupt railroads, it put together a 17,000 mile system which served seventeen states and two Canadian provinces. It became the second largest freight line in the country. By the end of that year, the new company had spent a billion dollars repairing about 12,000 freight cars and 500 locomotives, and rehabilitating worn out and dangerous tracks.

Since 1976 it has been estimated that the railroad was costing taxpayers $1,800,000 a day in subsidies, a staggering cost, but the railroad is vital to the economy of the middlewest and northeast states. Steel goes out from Pennsylvania, chemicals are shipped from Delaware, automobiles from Detroit, heavy machinery from Pittsburgh, coal from mines located in various areas, and many other essential goods move over Conrail's tracks.

It is doubtful that Conrail can be made profitable. It is burdened with labor agreements which require the employment of more workers than management feels it needs. The government indicated that it would like to carve up the system and and sell it off piecemeal to other railroads or business people interested in operating parts of it. In 1982 the prospects for any quick sale were dim and the administration was threatening to cut off further financial aid to the company.

In view of Conrail's uncertain future and the fact that it has had a labor surplus, it would not appear to be a good prospect for anyone seeking a railroading career at this time. You would be better advised to knock on the door of those railroads which are still operating independently and which have job openings from time to time.

THE MAJOR RAIL LINES

Although the future seemed clouded for Amtrak and Conrail, many of the larger stockholder-owned railroads were prospering in varying degrees. With past and contemplated mergers of large lines, the prospect of fewer but more efficient railroads was encouraging to many shippers. They are the lifeblood of railroads now that passenger service is operated mostly by Amtrak.

In 1980 Staggers Rail Act reduced much of the former government red tape and interference with railroad operation, making trains much more competitive with trucks and water carriers. It allowed railroads to sign long-term contracts in return for guaranteed volume which meant lower rates for the shippers and steady business for the carriers. Railroads could at last change their rates when necessary to meet the competition without waiting months or years for government approval. This change enabled them to attract business from the highways for the first time.

One area where this was especially beneficial was in the so-called *piggyback* business. This term refers to the movement of truck trailers and containers on rail flatcars. Instead of waiting for Interstate Commerce Commission permission to increase or lower rates for this kind of business, Conrail and the other roads can now match truck rates and initiate their own price changes daily, if necessary.

Just as some of the large truckers keep close track of their trucks, the railroads are improving their ability to spot freight cars wherever they may be. This is important to shippers who often must know where their goods are and when they will be delivered. More important, of course, is a railroad's ability to deliver the freight on schedule, when promised, and at costs competitive with other forms of ground transportation.

By the start of the 1980s it appeared that the railroads' share of total freight ton miles was growing and with it a rise in the companies' operating incomes. Increasing shipments of coal from mines in both the West and the East helped business. As some of the western carriers negotiated the purchase of oil and coal producing properties, economists forecast an even more profitable future for railroads.

One of the smaller but more interesting railroads worth noting, especially for the benefit of any readers who may be Alaskan buffs, is the Alaska Railroad which is owned by the federal government.

THE ALASKA RAILROAD

If you land at Seward, which is on Resurrection Bay, and plan to travel up to Fairbanks, undoubtedly you will want to go by rail. At the station your train of four modern coaches pulled by a diesel is waiting for you. At the conductor's signal the train starts off smoothly, proceeding inland to stop briefly at Portage, then wind around Cook Inlet and halt briefly at Anchorage to take on more passengers. From here the engine with its cars starts its long climb, passing eleven stations and crossing over the shoulder of Mount McKinley. Then it descends to the flats where the track leads into Fairbanks. It is a 470-mile, 12-hour winding trip through wilderness and if you look at a map of Alaska you will note that the Alaska Railroad serves only a very small part of the state. Nevertheless, the railroad's statistics are impressive:

Some 60,000 passengers ride each year between Anchorage and Fairbanks.

Approximately 100,000 people travel annually on the 12-mile branch line between Portage and Whittier. On this line trains disappear into a tunnel to pass beneath the Portage glacier. The railroad provides the only direct transportation between these two cities.

The federal government has indicated its desire to sell the railroad to the State of Alaska but the state officials replied that it would take the road only as a gift. Whatever the outcome, the railroad is an irreplaceable part of Alaska's transportation system and many Alaskans believe that the tracks should be extended to the Bering Sea. They see a railroad as the only acceptable form of transportation in a land of permafrost because the rails and their passing trains do not damage the environment.

During a recent year the railroad employed about 525 permanent employees and over 100 temporary workers for expanded maintenance of way programs during the few mild summer months. Of these, some forty were young Alaskan high school students acting as on-board tour guides providing hospitality to passengers. Although employment prospects are not encouraging, if railroading in such an environment interests you, write the Manager, Personnel, The Alaska Railroad, Pouch 7-2111, Anchorage, Alaska 99510.

SHORT-LINE RAILROADS

Short-line railroads, operated for tourists and/or railroad buffs, operate in various parts of the country. Probably the two best known are the Mount Washington and the Pikes Peak cog railways. These are seasonal operations which employ about two dozen men and women each. Many of them are college students interested in learning about railroading and earning money for their education. In addition, there are numerous restored rail lines over which steam or diesel power pulls a wide variety of equipment ranging from antique passenger cars to refurbished commuter coaches.

Most of the miniature roads are staffed by railroad buffs who work for the fun of it, but jobs on such lines provide experience as well as an opportunity to learn whether or not railroading if for you. If interested, write your state public utility commission for a list of such railroads and inquire about employment opportunities as early as possible.

What is undoubtedly the nation's most unusual railroad operates through the world's third longest railroad tunnel. The Henderson mine produces molybdenum ore some 5,000 feet and more below the peak of Red Mountain just east of the Continental Divide in Colorado. A short-line railroad takes the ore from the mine.

The double-track road starts deep within the mine at 7,500 feet above sea level where the ore cars are loaded. The electric powered trains proceed through the 9.6 mile tunnel to the portal where the tracks extend another 4.8 miles on the surface to the processing plant. Electric locomotives at each end of a train with two in the middle can power thirty ore cars. A round trip requires a little over an hour and a half.

About 1,900 men and women are employed at the mine which operates on a seven-day, around-the-clock schedule. Although there are numerous job opportunities in a variety of areas, those involved in transportation are quite limited. If you are interested, write: AMAX Inc., Public Relations, Henderson Mine, Empire, CO 80438.

RAILROAD WORKERS

In 1980 there were approximately 74,000 railroad brake operators, 47,000 locomotive engineers, and 33,000 railroad conductors, the three largest categories of rail employees. Altogether, the American railroads employed more than a half million workers whose jobs were divided into three separate categories: administrative, maintenance, and operating, or transportation.

The once-familiar sight of a veteran engineer leaning out the cab window, his hand on the throttle and his eyes straining ahead to see the next signal, inspired many a boy to become a locomotive engineer. Then airplane pilots replaced steam locomotive engineers as heroes for young boys. The advent of the diesel locomotive further eroded the romantic appeal of railroading. Nevertheless, the haunting train whistle echoing through the valley to the pounding of the heavy driving wheels is not altogether gone either.

Equal employment opportunity means that now you can look up at the cab of a speeding diesel and possibly see a woman at the throttle. Today railroading is open to everyone and while the nostalgia of the old steam engine is gone, some young people are attracted to the prospect of running diesel and electric engines.

Many look with equal enthusiasm at the career possibilities which exist elsewhere in railroad companies. Against this background let's see what employment opportunities there may be for you in the three principal divisions of a railroad. Space limitations make it necessary to sketch the positions briefly.

Administrative

Railroads are no different from other industries which require a wide variety of clerical and other office personnel. Accordingly you will find the usual secretaries and clerks performing specialized duties. Then there are employees working in the advertising, computer, labor relations, legal, personnel, public relations, purchasing, and sales departments. Other specialists are scattered throughout the entire organization.

Maintenance

Making certain that engines, freight and passenger cars, as well as tracks, signals, and communications equipment are in perfect working order is the responsibility of this division. Because trains operate around the clock, continuous attention must be paid to every part of the operation.

Included among the specialized jobs in this division is that of car repairer. That person may be assigned to check rolling stock as it comes into a terminal, or work in the repair shop performing necessary maintenance or major overhaul. Mechanics are assigned to diesel engines and other motorized equipment while electricians repair and service electrical equipment in locomotives and cars. They also work on air conditioners and other electrical apparatuses. A variety of skilled workers make repairs on motors, engine and car frames; replace parts such as fuel lines, air hoses, valves, and wheels; or rebuild engine transmissions.

Out on the right-of-way, gangs of workers replace rails and ties and tamp down ballast to keep tracks in top condition. Others repair and paint bridges, clean culverts, and dig ditches alongside the roadbed. Much of this work is now performed by intricate machinery which decreases the need for the large section gangs. Some employees are required to operate the machines however.

Communications are important to safe operations. Trained maintenance workers service the all-important signal system. They also repair the telephone, radio and microwave systems. Radio is used so that engineers can talk with their conductors a mile away in the caboose, and personnel can communicate with each other in the yards and between stations.

Transportation

These are the men and women who run the trains: engineers, brake operators (formerly called brakemen), and conductors. In the days of the coal-fired steam engines, a fireman was an important member of the engine crew. With the advent of diesels, the services of a fireman were eliminated.

Engineers operate locomotives in passenger, freight, or yard service. Passenger trains run on tight schedules and it is the engineer's job to reach each station on time. If the train is delayed by red signals or for other reasons, he or she tries to make up for lost time but without sacrificing safety.

Freight engineers pilot freight trains which may be either through fast freights operating on set schedules or local freights which pick up and drop cars at way stations. They too operate according to a schedule, but are not necessarily held to it because the number of cars to be switched varies from day to day.

Yard engineers who run the switching engines make up trains by sorting out cars and pulling or pushing them to the tracks where they will be coupled together to form new trains.

Brake operators ride on the trains, one in the caboose with the conductor, the other up in front in the cab with the engineer. In the old days before the air brake was invented, brakemen were what their name implies. They operated the hand brakes on freight and passenger cars on a signal from the engineer. It was dangerous work, running back and forth on top of swaying freight cars in icy or snowy weather. It is still dangerous because when a freight train approaches a siding to pick up or drop cars, the brake operator jumps off the engine and runs ahead to set the switches.

The brake operator also couples and uncouples cars at terminals, stations, and sidings. In the yards the brake operator couples and uncouples cars, and throws switches. He or she often climbs up a car to ride with it and control its speed with the hand brake as it rolls down an incline to be joined with a series of cars that are being made up into a train.

Brake operators on passenger trains have it much easier. They watch over the operation of the cars and their equipment. They also use flags and flares to protect the train from a rear end collision whenever the train is forced to make an unscheduled stop.

Conductors are in charge of trains, whether passenger, freight, or yard. The yard conductors supervise the men and make up trains.

Working Conditions

Most train crew members do not have a regular five-day week. Railroad assignments are made on the basis of seniority. The more years you have worked, the more you have to say about when you want to work. New employees may be on call twenty-four hours a day, never knowing when they will be called to report for duty.

Those employed in the office, the shops, and out on the tracks usually have regular shifts. During the snow months section gangs may work overtime clearing the switches and tracks. In the event of an accident or other emergency they may be called out to work nights and weekends.

Education and Training

A high school diploma is the minimum educational requirement for the majority of railroad jobs. One of the best things about railroading is that in most assignments you learn on the job and may be taught by a skilled worker.

For the jobs in the maintenance and transportation division some railroads seek trained applicants. Others train you on the job, depending on the position.

Conductors are chosen from the ranks of brake operators. Engineers may serve first as engineers' helpers to obtain training, and then take substitute assignments as engineers. Engineers must have sufficient knowledge of train service rules to pass an examination on the operation of diesel or electric locomotives.

To qualify for their jobs, conductors, brake operators, and engineers must be able to pass examinations showing that they have satisfactory hearing, eyesight and color vision, as well as ability to exercise good judgment. Once employed in these positions they must be able to pass periodic physical exams.

Railroads at present are not the best source of jobs in the transportation field because they are not growing as some industries are. Nevertheless, if you are eager to carve out a career in this business (which dates back to 1830 and has achieved tremendous importance and growth since then) there is every reason why you should investigate the possibilities of finding an entry job.

For further information write the Office of Information and Public Affairs, Association of American Railroads, 1920 L Street, NW, Washington, DC 20036, and ask for a copy of their career publication: *The Human Side of Railroading.*

A metrobus operator in Washington D.C. gives directions to help passengers, in addition to keeping up on traffic and weather conditions, changing regulations, equipment, and road conditions, and the main job of driving the route. (Photo: Paul Myatt, WMATA.)

CHAPTER 9

CAREERS IN
PUBLIC TRANSIT

At the turn of the century it was possible to travel all the way between New York and Boston by electric trolley, if you had the time and the patience to make the innumerable changes required. What is more, it was said that one might go most of the way from New York to Chicago via local trolleys and interurban lines. It was a time when trolley fever gripped the whole country and even small towns laid single track lines with turnouts every so often to permit the cars to pass.

Trolleys took commuters to work, housewives to market, the wealthy to the opera, children to school and Sunday school picnics, and vacationers to amusement parks or sparkling lakes. As long as there were passengers to fill the seats of the swaying cars this was a relatively inexpensive, safe, and dependable way to travel.

Webster's dictionary defines transit as "local transportation, especially of people by public conveyance." Our story here starts when the trolley era gave way to the automobile and then the bus.

Once the public had discovered the convenience of owning an automobile, many people gradually abandoned the trolley, especially in small towns. Later, the development of bigger buses for use in cities and large towns provided greater convenience and safety for passengers. They could board or leave the vehicles at the curb rather than in the middle of the street where trolley tracks had to be. Then "Trackless Trolleys" were developed to give the trolley cars greater flexibility, but the cars still had to draw current from overhead wires which were supported by unsightly poles.

As cities grew, trolleys were unable to handle the growing number of passengers traveling into and within urban areas. Subways were dug to supplement the surface transportation. Today, although trolleys have disappeared altogether from New York and many other cities, you can ride one in Boston where they are still used, along with buses and subway trains within a coordinated transit system.

Elsewhere America's most unusual trolley cars are undoubtedly San Francisco's, which are as much a part of that city as the steep hills for which their endless cables and quaint cars were constructed. In 1982 the ancient system was closed for a two-year overhaul, much to the sorrow of many regular passengers and visitors to the city. The cars were not the most efficient form of transportation but they were invaluable as a tourist attraction for the city.

The trolley is not entirely a thing of the past, however. It is making a comeback in a slightly different form from earlier versions. One of the first new lines, the "Tijuana Trolley," opened in July 1981. It glides down sixteen miles of abandoned track and right-of-way between San Diego, California, and the Mexican border.

Fourteen electric trolley cars were expected to carry 10,000 riders a day as they made their 18 stops along the way, but the management was amazed when some 11,500 passengers clamored to board the cars and soon their number grew to 18,000. The line proved so successful that another 17-mile trolley line was planned for the benefit of residents living in San Diego's eastern suburbs.

Far to the east, in Buffalo, a 6.4 mile light rail system with 14 stations was pushing out from downtown to the State University of New York campus, the first part of an ambitious multiphase plan.

Meanwhile Los Angeles was working on a design to build a midtown elevated railroad, an overhead electric "people mover." Similar lines were being projected in Detroit and Miami. Enormously expensive to build, 80 percent of the cost would be paid for by the Urban Mass Transportation Agency which is concerned with helping cities solve their transportation problems.

Subways are not a thing of the past either. In the 60s, San Francisco built its extensive BART, Bay Area Rapid Transit System. Atlanta opened the first 7.1 miles of its projected 53-mile MARTA system in September 1979. But the most ambitious new subway opened its first 4.6 miles of track on March 29, 1976, when the Washington Metropolitan Area Transit Authority dispatched its first train on what would eventually be a 98-mile system. Here, as in San Diego, the public's response exceeded all expectations. Some 21,000 passengers were boarding at the 5 stations of the planned 86-station system, 21,000 men, women, and children, compared to the anticipated 8,000!

Subways provide only part of essential transport services because surface transportation is equally vital to the needs of travelers within an urban area. As already mentioned, most of the urban and suburban transport service is provided by buses. Yet we should not overlook the trolleys, subways, and light rail trains which are also important to any transit system. The light rail trains operate principally in a limited-stop service such as is offered in San Diego or Buffalo.

The introduction of computers and other automatic devices by the newer transit systems is making these organizations most interesting places to work. A brief look at the new Washington Metro system will suggest a few of the innovations which are making some transit careers so intriguing.

WASHINGTON METRO

The Washington Metro was established in 1966 to plan, construct, finance, and provide for the operation of a rapid rail and bus transit system for the Washington Metropolitan Area. It was to be managed by elected officials from the District of Columbia, Maryland, and Virginia.

From the very beginning it was decided that the bus and rail systems would complement, not compete with each other. Buses would take riders to outlying Metro stations.

As the rail system continues to expand, the bus routes will be coordinated with it. The local governments whose representatives manage the Metro set the level of bus service in their areas, where and how often the buses run, thus determining how much or how little they want to provide their taxpayers.

Metrobus

The Metrobus system, which operates a fleet of approximately 1,800 buses, complements the rail service with its 392 basic bus routes and some 800 route variations, making it the fourth largest bus system in the country. All of the buses are equipped with two-way radios, silent radio alarms, flashing lights for protection, and air-conditioning for comfort.

In the communications center, radio dispatchers are constantly on duty providing two-way communication with each Metrobus operating in the region. This enables the dispatcher to adjust quickly to any unexpected crisis, such as an accident. A silent alarm built into the radio system enables police to respond to an operator's signal for help.

The system has eight modern bus garages for the storage, maintenance, and repair of its vehicles. Most of these are located in the outer suburbs to give more efficient service to the Maryland and Virginia passengers, since many of the bus lines act as feeders into the Metro trains.

Metro Trains

This is how the Metro describes its automatic train system:

"People, backed up by highly sophisticated communications and control equipment, run Metro.

"Safety, efficiency, and security were prime considerations in the selections of an advanced wayside control system, computer-assisted control center, radio communication, a 2,000-line capacity private telephone network, system-wide public address systems, TV surveillance network, and a failsafe system for nearly every conceivable equipment malfunction or human error.

"Although trains operate automatically in normal service, a well-trained operator sits at the control console, opens and closes doors, announces upcoming stations, communicates with central control, informs passengers of items that may affect their trip, takes manual control of the train at a moment's notice, and performs scores of other duties.

"He takes orders from the supervisors in central control, but, like the captain of a ship, he bears firstline responsibility for the well-being of his passengers, which may number more than 1,500 on an eight-car train during peak periods."

Here is a description of the control room:

"Control room supervisors, having an electronic overview of the entire Metro system, make and implement decisions to keep it running smoothly.

"The operations control center, located in the Metro headquarters building, is the hub of the vast Metro communications and control network.

"Control room supervisors perform three major tasks: taking corrective action as problems occur, dispatching repair crews for equipment malfunctions or failures, and performing emergency communications.

"When trains fail to move as they should, the supervisors choose and execute a solution after considering a list of options. When a malfunction occurs, the supervisors know whom to call to fix it. In an emergency, the supervisor summons help via police and fire hot lines.

"Train control supervisors operate two push-button consoles, one for train operations and the other for Metro support systems. Eight CRT (TV) screens arranged in two horizontal rows face the consoles. The supervisor at the train operations console monitors and controls train movement. The supervisor at the other console handles problems with support systems such as the electrical substations, station air-conditioning, tunnel ventilation, drainage, station fire and intrusion alarms, and other facilities.

"Support system failures appear as alarms on the CRT screens, or they are called in by station attendants.

"The train operations supervisor uses the CRT screens as electronic windows to view schematic representations of tracks, trains, and stations throughout the Metro system. Displays on the screen show tracks, cross-overs, turnouts, pocket tracks, stations, and moving trains. As the train (shown in triangles moving along the track lines) enters the station (shown as open rectangles), the rectangles are filled in to show that the train in the station has its doors open.

"If a train falls behind schedule by more than a minute, an alarm flashes on the screen showing the time when the train fell behind. By asking the computers via the console, the supervisor learns the complete history of the train's movement for the last five stations, enabling him to find the cause of the current delay. He may keep hands-off and allow the computer to correct the delay, which is one of its programmed functions. He may also execute a plan in which some of the trains ahead and some behind the slow train will mimic its movements in sequence, thus maintaining constant spacing."

All transit systems are not as automated as Washington's but many of the newer ones have incorporated numerous electronic and fail-safe systems to protect their passengers. Even the older systems like those in Boston, Chicago, and New York are gradually adopting many of these innovations but it is difficult and expensive to modernize these older subway and bus operations.

JOB OPPORTUNITIES

In the transit sector of transportation the greatest number of jobs are for bus drivers. In fact in 1980 there were approximately 97,000 bus drivers employed mostly in large cities. The majority of them worked for transit lines. A few were also employed by schools, churches, commercial interests, and sightseeing companies.

Driving Occupations

Most experienced drivers have regularly scheduled runs but new drivers are usually placed on an "extra" list to substitute for regular drivers who are ill or on vacation. They may also be assigned to extra and special runs, for example during morning or evening rush hours, or to stadiums when there are special sporting events. In some cities or towns transit buses transport school children to and from school and extra list drivers may operate these buses. New drivers remain on the extra list until they have enough seniority to get a regular run which may take several years.

Promotional opportunities are limited but experienced drivers can rise to jobs as dispatchers or supervisors, and eventually to management positions. Dispatchers assign buses to drivers, make sure drivers are on schedule, reroute buses when necessary, and dispatch extra buses and drivers whenever there is an accident or breakdown and additional vehicles are needed.

To apply for a position as a bus driver you should be at least twenty-one years old, be in good health, have good eyesight, with or without glasses, and have a good driving record. A number of employers prefer applicants who have a high school education or its equivalent. The majority require applicants to pass a physical examination and a written test showing they can follow complex bus schedules. Most states require bus drivers to have a chauffeur's license which is a commercial driving permit. Drivers face many minor annoyances such as difficult passengers, traffic tie-ups, bad weather, and fatigue. A relaxed personality is important for this work.

Operators of trolleys and subway trains will find that most of the above qualifications apply to them as well but specific requirements will vary from city to city. Training is received on the job as is the case with engineers on railroads, and in some systems it may take years before you will be on a regular run.

Note: If you apply for a position with a publicly owned bus or transit system—and most of them are—you will find that all of the jobs are under civil service. This means that appointment to a position and later promotion may depend on your taking a competitive civil service examination.

Other Transit Jobs

Next to driving occupations, probably the most number of jobs will be found in the maintenance and repair shops of buses, trolleys, and subways. All vehicles must be kept in top running condition and since most of them are used practically every day they must get frequent checks and maintenance. They are also taken out of service periodically for major repairs. All this work is usually performed by employees of the transit companies.

Cleaners, mechanics, electricians, welders, painters, upholsterers, and glaziers are some of the specialists needed to keep a fleet of transit buses and trains moving. Your best way to prepare for such openings is to take special training at a trade school.

In most cities transit service operates late into the evening or all night, as is the case in New York City. As a new worker, you will probably be assigned to the night or late shift. As you get seniority, you will be able to bid for better and perhaps more regular working hours.

In the office of any transit company you will find the usual clerical, computer, and receptionist type positions. In addition, there are those posts which call for specialized or college training. You will find such positions in the sales, purchasing, public relations, planning, finance, and budget departments. Although turnover in these administrative offices is not likely to be high, investigate the opportunities anyway.

Advantages and Disadvantages

Here are some compelling reasons why you should enter this field if it interests you:

1. Most jobs are open to everyone because they are under your local municipal or other civil service system. This means that all people including minorities are guaranteed equal consideration for positions.
2. There are good chances for promotion because many of these systems are large. Those with college degrees and/or many years of experience may be in line for promotion to supervisory and managerial posts.
3. Benefits are greater than in many other fields. The overtime, pensions, sick leave, health care, and paid vacations are more generous than in most industries.
4. There is better than average job security, especially after you have been on the job several years.

On the other hand every job has its drawbacks and you should be prepared to face these possible disadvantages:

CHAPTER 10

CAREERS IN THE PIPELINE INDUSTRY

Even before Edwin L. Drake made his famous discovery of oil on his Titusville farm in 1859, barrels of brine oil were being transported from wells in Tarentum, Pennsylvania, to distant points by wagon, boats, and railroad. The cooperage industry enjoyed a sudden boom with the demand for barrels, but it was only six years after the black liquid was discovered that the pipeline industry was born.

In western Pennsylvania Sam Van Syckel laid six miles of two-inch pipe from the Pithold Field to the nearest railroad station at Miller's Farm. Now oil could be transported to the railroad at a saving of fifty cents a barrel. Soon other railroads wanted their share of the new business and additional pipelines were built to carry oil to their tracks. The price competition brought rates down below the Van Syckel costs and two years later this original company went bankrupt.

This did not deter further development of pipelines, however. In 1869 Tidewater laid the first long distance line from Coryville in the oil producing region, all the way to Williamsport. Now some 6,000 barrels of crude were flowing each day through the 108-mile, six-inch pipe up over the Allegheny Mountains. The competition between this and other early lines became so intense that rates for carrying oil dropped to the point where the railroads gave up soliciting long-haul crude oil transportation. Since that time pipelines have been laid throughout the world until today most of the world's oil now travels by pipeline from wells to distant tank farms.

THE DEVELOPING PIPELINE BUSINESS

Although pipelines were rarely if ever seen by the public, they are an important part of our transportation system, carrying 24 percent of all inter-city freight. Looking at it another way, the 200,000 miles of pipeline total a bit more than all the miles of main line railroad right-of-way. This vast system consists of two types of pipes: those which deliver crude oil to the refineries; and the smaller "products" pipelines which carry items such as kerosine or gasoline from the refineries. They deliver about 35 percent of all refined petroleum products sold in the United States.

Pipelines provide the cheapest and most efficient method of overland transportation. Because they are laid mostly underground, there is little wear and tear on the pipe. Not only is it protected from the elements but vandalism as well. Its power sources, pumps and compressors, are stationery, and best of all, it is free of the unprofitable "return trip" which is required of railroad cars, trucks, or boats. Pipelines do not require handling, containers, terminals, or the need to keep extra vehicles or boats on hand to cover a breakdown or other emergency.

When oil was discovered in the Oklahoma and Texas fields during the early 1900s, no one even considered transporting the crude oil by railroad. Companies laid pipelines directly from the wells to refineries and tanker loading ports on the Gulf Coast. Soon sections of pipe were reaching Chicago and the upper Midwest. During the early 1920s the first crude was flowing to the Midwest from the Rocky Mountain area. These lines were usually eight-inch or smaller because larger pipe could not withstand high pressures. If greater capacity was needed, dual pipes would be laid side by side, but the 1930s changed all that.

High-strength and seamless pipe permitted companies to use lines of greater diameter than eight–twelve inches. Although the larger pipe was more economical to operate, it proved more costly to build. Furthermore, it required more volume to fill than most refiners could provide; hence, two or more companies would join together to build these larger lines, enabling them to meet their total demand.

Oil is moved through pipelines by pumps which push it along at the Chicago Corporation, which owned a large natural gas reserve, was seeking a market for its underground surplus.

At the request of the War Production Board the Federal Power Commission issued a certificate permitting construction of a natural gas pipeline from South Texas to West Virginia. The authorization was issued in September 1943 to a new subsidiary of the Chicago Corporation called Tennessee Gas and Transmission. In making the authorization the War Production Board had stipulated that the 1,265-mile long pipeline must be completed for operation during the winter of 1944–45.

The fledgling Tennessee Gas and Transmission Company had to assemble an organization, find the necessary materials, hire survey-ors and workers to prepare 1,265 miles of right-of-way, let contracts, and construct the twenty-four-inch pipeline, all in record time in order to meet the deadline. They had to do all this at a time when materials and labor were practically unobtainable.

The first payroll was set up on October 1, 1943, with only a few names on it. Only five weeks after these first employees started work, all but one of the construction contracts had been let. On December 4 ground was broken at the Cumberland River in Tennessee, and the first mainline pipe was welded less than a month later.

The work had scarcely begun, however, before bad weather set in. By May 1 only 76 miles or roughly six percent of the 1,265-mile pipeline had been built. The heavy rain in construction areas turned normally workable terrain into impassible and impossible quag-mires. Rocky and mountainous terrain and material shortages added to the mounting problems.

Summer brought improved weather and an increase in the con-struction pace. In spite of the difficulties and the slow start, the company met its deadline. Gas began moving through the new pipe-line on October 31, 1944, less than 11 months from the start of construction. Tennessee Gas had laid more than 1,200 miles of pipeline during wartime, most of it in the last six months at a rate of nearly 7 miles a day. It had secured right-of-way permits from thousands of landowners, crossed 67 rivers and hundreds of roads, highways, and railroads, and built seven pipeline compressor sta-tions. Natural gas, which would have gone unused or been wasted in Texas and Louisiana for lack of a market, was being burned in Appalachian factories where it was badly needed. Tennessee Gas had become an operating company.

In 1966 the company's name was changed to Tenneco Inc. Today the subsidiary, which bears the company's former corporate name, Tennessee Gas Transmission Company, provides overall administrative and staff services for Tenneco's pipeline network of more than 16,000 miles, over 1.5 million compressor horsepower, in systems operated by four companies.

That original single line has grown into one of the nation's largest interstate pipeline systems, serving utility companies in twenty-five states. More than 85 percent of the gas consumers in Tenneco's populous service area are high priority users—residences, hospitals, schools, and small commercial enterprises. In order to keep these users well-supplied, the company has traditionally relied on the natural gas producing areas of the Gulf Coast. However, existing reserves of gas are declining and the company is therefore working to develop new reserves. This decline in the nation's domestic reserves of conventional gas is a harsh reality but the company, and others in the gas industry, are devoting every effort to develop additional supplies.

One major source of natural gas is the Prudhoe Bay area in northern Alaska. A pipeline was authorized to run south from Prudhoe Bay parallel to the Alaskan oil pipeline to Fairbanks, then east to the Canadian border to join a Canadian-built pipeline extending to the American border. Here one branch would head toward San Francisco and the other to Chicago in order to serve the upper Midwest.

In 1983 it appeared that the pipeline might never be built. The principal reasons were the high construction costs, the cost of the delivered gas which could not compete with gas sold by other pipeline companies, the difficulty in finding investors for the project, and disagreements over obtaining right-of-way permits through Alaska. Perhaps at some future time, when other supplies of oil, coal, and gas become depleted, this pipeline will become as necessary to the nation as the one Tennessee Gas and Transmission Company laid during World War II.

PIPELINE TRANSPORTATION JOBS

There are more than 3,000 separate occupations in the petroleum industry but we are concerned here only with those which pertain to pipeline transportation.

Here are the specialist occupations Amoco lists together with the training required for each: (See footnote on page 114 for code.)

Aircraft Patrol Pilot (A)
Aircraft Mechanic (B)
Carpenter Foreman (A)
Chemist (XB)
Chief Deliveryman (A)
Chief Operator (Pump Station) (A)
Civil Engineer (XA)
Connection Foreman (A)
Corrosion Engineer (XA)
Electrician (A)
Foreman (A)
Gager (C) and (D)
Lineman (B)
Loader (D)
Material and Warehouse Supervisor (B)
Mechanic (A)
Mechanical Engineer (XA)
Operator (B)
Operator (Metering Station) (A)
Pipeline Construction Inspector (A)
Pipeline Crew Foreman (A)
Radio Technician (B)
Right-of-Way and Claims Agent (A)
Shop Foreman (A)
Station Superintendent (A)
Supervisor - Radio Communication (A)
Tank Foreman (A)
Terminal Man (C)
Tester (Laboratory) (C)
Welder (B)

Welder Foreman (A)
Work Equipment Operator (C)

Amoco Pipeline Company operates 15,700 miles of pipeline, extending from Utah in the west to Indiana in the east, and north and south from the Canadian border and to the Gulf of Mexico. The company is a subsidiary of Standard Oil Company (Indiana) and is responsible for transporting petroleum and petroleum products from oil fields and refineries to markets. Discoveries of new fields, declines of older ones, and changes in marketing requirements mean constant changes for the system, as new pipeline is added and existing lines are modernized and revised.

If you are considering an engineering career Amoco Pipeline needs engineers of various disciplines to handle pipeline construction and operations according to a company spokesperson. They are interested primarily in holders of bachelors of science degrees in mechanical, electrical and civil engineering. Typical assignments include evaluations for new facilities, such as crude oil gathering systems, cross-country pipelines, pumping stations, metering installations and tankage. Their engineers are responsible for electrical and mechanical design, development of material and construction specifications, supervision and inspection of construction, and supervision of operations.

Two typical pipeline positions are those of dispatcher and inspector. Here are brief descriptions of each:

Dispatchers watch over and regulate the flow of natural gas in the

---

Code: A. Work requiring a high degree of precision, long experience, knowledge of intricate machine operations, special education or unusual aptitude. B. Work requiring one year or longer in training, and involving any or all of the following: precision, accuracy, familiarity with specified basic processes, or special education. C. Work requiring between six months and one year of training before a new worker is qualified with respect to skill, reliability, or production. D. Work requiring less than six months of training before a new or upgraded employee is competent. X. Jobs which require four years of college training in a recognized professional school.

pipelines. Sitting before an instrument panel, they can tell how much oil or gas is passing through the pipe as well as its temperature, pressure, and speed. In the case of gas, they may have to decide how much will be needed by customers during the next few hours so there will be an ample supply on hand. They do this after taking into consideration the outside temperature and expected weather conditions, the time of day, and past needs. Then they change the flow by adjusting switches which open or close valves and regulate the speed of compressors, all of which may be located many miles away. In the event of an emergency they must make quick decisions and take appropriate action. Some dispatchers stationed at the end of oil pipelines are responsible for routing the crude through smaller lines to the storage tanks of their numerous customers. Promotion may be to the job of chief dispatcher. This person supervises dispatchers, does long-range planning for the movements of gas or oil through the pipelines and keeps various records of the operation for departmental accounts, government reports, and other uses.

Inspectors use test equipment as they travel along the pipelines looking for leaks or signs of other problems. Depending on the terrain, they either drive a truck which contains their equipment or walk along the buried or above-ground pipe searching for signs of leaks. Some companies use airplanes to patrol those above-ground lines which run through remote areas. In cities inspectors' work is more complicated as they watch over pipes which run under streets and sidewalks and branch into buildings.

It goes without saying that although the list of Amoco specialist positions did not include the usual office positions open to clerical, financial, sales, public relations, purchasing, and legal personnel, they are as essential to any pipeline company as the engineers, dispatchers, or inspectors.

EMPLOYMENT OUTLOOK

Prospects for employment in this industry are quite promising. The natural gas industry is the sixth largest employer in the country and since both the gas and oil industries are essential to the nation's

Frequent inspections help prevent leakage. (Photo: DuPont.)

welfare, they are not affected by recessions as much as most industries. Pay scales are generally high, employee benefits generous, and working conditions on the whole good. Pipelines are the most important means of delivering gas and oil from wells to customers or refineries. Remember, though, that there are additional employment possibilities with oil companies since petroleum products are also transported by ship, railroad tank cars, and tank trucks. Although petroleum is not found in every state, practically every city and town has a distributor of oil or petroleum products and distribution means transportation.

High school graduates have better chances of finding beginning jobs than those who cannot produce a diploma. If you have had some related part-time experience during summer vacations, it should prove helpful in finding a job. Many companies have their own training programs for new employees but if you have obtained some technical training, you will find it advantageous when you interview for a job.

Consult the following periodicals for possible advertisements of job openings: *Butane Propane News, LP-Gas News, National Petroleum News,* and the *Oil and Gas Journal.* If your library does not have subscriptions to them, perhaps you could ask to see issues at the office of your nearest gas or oil distributor. Be sure to contact local employment agencies and your state employment security office.

For futher information write the American Petroleum Institute, 2101 L Street, NW, Washington, DC 20037; American Gas Association, 1515 Wilson Boulevard, Arlington, VA 22209; or the Association of Oil Pipe Lines, 1725 K Street, NW, Washington, DC 20006.

Diesel cabs are being used to conserve fuel in some urban areas.
(Photo: Peugeot News, Liason Agency, NYC.)

CHAPTER 11

AUTOMOBILE-RELATED CAREERS

TAXICABS

"We always talked taxicabs at home. I guess it was in my blood."

Allen Kaplan leaned back in his desk chair and recalled his childhood which revolved about his grandfather Baron's business. Cab Operating Company was a family affair which Sol Baron started in the Greenpoint section of Brooklyn, New York, in 1926.

In the beginning, he bought one car and hired a driver to operate it. He was a mechanic and made certain the cab was always in good running order. After he added more cars, Fannie, his wife, became the dispatcher, telling the drivers where to go, checking their reports, and making certain they did not cheat the company. The Barons discovered that the taxi business is a seven-day-a-week, around-the-clock responsibility and is busiest at holiday times like Christmas Eve, New Year's Eve, and Easter.

When Allen was in college he considered studying law, but he had taxicabs in his blood. He decided to go into his grandfather's business. On the company's 75th anniversary in 1981, Cab Operating, one of the 19 remaining fleets in New York City, owned 80 cars, and enjoyed a good reputation with the Taxi and Limousine Commission which regulates taxi cabs in that metropolis.

In a city like New York taxi regulation is strict. The number of cabs which cruise the streets, free to pick up fares on demand, is limited. Another group of cabs may respond only to telephone calls,

119

but in Rumney, New Hampshire, a tiny town, anyone who has a car, a chauffeur's license, and proper insurance can operate a taxi service.

If this business interests you, perhaps you can start your career as a driver for a fleet of cabs or a small company. You will probably work either the day shift which starts anywhere between 6:00 A.M. and 8:00 A.M., or the night shift which may begin the minute a cab arrives back at the garage between 3:00 P.M. and 5:00 P.M. As soon as the car is gassed and cleaned, you drive it out and when you return is entirely up to you as long as the car is back in time for the day shift.

Driving a taxi is an uncertain occupation. If you are in a large city you must learn where to cruise or wait for the best fares. If you live in a smaller city or town, you probably will receive your jobs at the taxi office which takes all the taxi requests by phone. Here you must sit and wait for a call because there would be no point cruising to find business.

In some cities the job can be hazardous, especially if you must drive into high crime areas. No two days will ever be alike. Your income will depend on tips and in addition you may receive between 40 and 50 percent of the fares you collect. It can be a long day's work, you may or may not be busy, and you could find it tiring to sit behind the wheel all that time. On the other hand, many drivers would not trade their jobs because they enjoy the freedom plus the element of surprise.

Although a high school diploma may not be necessary to land a job as a taxi driver, you should have taken a driver education course, and have a chauffeur's license. In some cities you may need a permit to drive as well. Check with your motor vehicle office for the requirements in your area and inquire about job prospects at the office of each taxi company.

LIMOUSINE DRIVERS

You may live in an area where there is a demand for chauffeurs. Unlike taxi drivers who are at the beck and call of the public, limousine chauffeurs or drivers work for one employer: a business which has a car to drive officers and other employees to distant points;

government agencies which must provide transportation for some of their top administrators; resorts; private schools; car rental agencies which might need you to drive cars from the rental office to the garage and back; and livery companies which rent chauffeur-driven limousines to wealthy customers.

Some chauffeurs may be hired by people who prefer to be driven in their own cars. Other chauffeurs own their own cars which they drive for customers who have special transportation needs.

Chauffeurs must have a chauffeur's license. They usually wear a uniform or a dark business suit, and should be well mannered, attentive, and ready to render various small services and courtesies to their employers.

SERVICE STATION EMPLOYEES

Although there is a growing trend toward self-service gasoline stations, even at those stations where customers fill their own tanks there must be attendants to take the money and make certain the pumps are operating satisfactorily. There are still many other service stations where attendants man the pumps, clean the windshields, and check the oil.

Such service stations also employ mechanics to repair and service cars. If a mechanic's job is interesting to you, you might start working at the gas pumps and then ask to be given assignments in the shop repairing flat tires, changing oil, lubricating, or checking brake linings. If you have the ability you might become a junior mechanic working under an experienced man. Should the station have a tow truck, you might be responsible for answering emergency calls and bringing disabled vehicles to the station.

CAR RENTAL AGENCIES

The rack of a car rental office in a large city was jammed with reservations folders, the name of the renter written in black crayon across the top of each. Some of the names included R. Reagan, B.

Bunny, Ronstadt and Wonder. These were fake reservations used because there were not enough real customers and the manager wanted to make it appear that the office was busy. The situation was typical of much of the industry at the beginning of the 1980s, although some of the companies, like Budget Car Rental, were doing well. Business in this industry, like many others, can fluctuate widely because much of it depends on the people who travel on business or pleasure and when airline traffic is down, car rental activity drops off too.

Car rental companies are found at every airport of any size, in downtown areas of cities, as well as in some suburbs and many small towns. At the reservations counters agents take reservations by phone or in person. These clerks fill out the necessary forms, telephone the garage for vehicles, and make certain that each customer understands the terms of the rental agreement. Drivers bring the cars from the garage and take them back when they are returned. At the garage, mechanics keep the cars in top running order while cleaners make certain they are immaculate inside and out.

A high school diploma will qualify you for simple clerical positions which may be available. Qualifications for mechanics were mentioned in the previous section while openings for cleaners or other unskilled labor would be available on a first come basis regardless of your educational attainments.

Many high schools offer automotive repair courses as do vocational or technical schools. With this training you will be far more useful to the service station owner than the applicant who has no skills. Good mechanics are usually in demand, the work is varied and interesting, and the pay is good.

PARKING ATTENDANTS

In most cities and large towns parking lots are a necessity for storing the automobiles which are driven into the crowded business districts. Although it is estimated that 90 percent of the parking lots and garages have automatic toll collectors, there are many which hire attendants to park cars. In some large parking garages attendants drive the cars up ramps or onto elevators which lift them to whatever floor has parking space available.

DRIVING INSTRUCTORS

Public schools and private driving schools employ driving intructors who teach their students while driving in dual-control training cars.

Requirements for this job vary from state to state but you should be a high school graduate, at least twenty-one years old, have a driver's license, and a good driving record. Inquire at your local board of education and the office of commercial driving schools regarding possible openings.

For further information contact International Taxicab Association, 11300 Rockville Pike, Rockville, MD 20852; Automotive Information Council, 28333 Telegraph Road, Southfield, MI 48034; National Parking Association, Inc., 1101 Seventeenth Street, NW, Washington, DC 20036; American Driver and Traffic Safety Education Association, 1201 Sixteenth Street, NW, Washington, DC 20036.

Overleaf: Checking baggage is an essential job that must be done in nearly every terminal. (Photo: United Air Lines.)

CHAPTER 12

CAREERS IN TERMINALS AND TRAVEL AGENCIES

TERMINALS

Any weekday at five o'clock visit Seattle's ferry terminal, one of Chicago's commuter railroad terminals, or the mammoth New York Port Authority Bus Terminal. As you watch the thousands of men and women rushing to catch ferries, planes, trains, or buses you will realize what busy and important places terminals can be. Even the small terminal in Vermont's White River Junction which serves Greyhound and Vermont Transit buses can be a hectic place as frantic passengers run up to the single window for tickets or information and the loud speaker blares "Last call for New York City on platform three." The difference between this terminal and the one in New York is a matter of size, but the operations and problems are similar.

What is a terminal? Simply stated it is a place from which passengers, freight, and express depart and arrive. Whatever form of transportation it may serve, a terminus must supply facilities for loading and unloading passengers and freight, and in the case of a passenger terminal, provide waiting rooms, restaurant and comfort facilities, as well as ready access to ground transportation. In addition it should be possible to fuel, clean, provision, and repair the planes, trains, vehicles, or ships. Thus a wide range of workers is needed to provide all the service required.

The organization and management of terminals vary widely. At a large airport each airline may have its own terminal which is part of the overall complex. At a small airport the terminal may serve two or three airlines but have a consolidated ticket office with baggage handlers, mechanics, and fleet service workers. These workers are employees of the terminal company. Some bus terminals offer consolidated services with two or more lines using the facilities. In the case of railroads or ferries, where usually only one carrier arrives and departs, one group of employees provides all the necessary services.

Whatever the arrangements, they are of little consequence to you if you are investigating career possibilities at a terminal. However, you should bear in mind that if you are a mechanic, for example, you might find that the terminal management has no such job openings because each of the carriers uses its own employees. On the other hand, were you interested in a reservations or ticketing position, you might learn that the terminal company provides these services to all the carriers, and it is the place to apply. The best way to discover what job openings there are is to visit the terminal's personnel office.

We have already covered the career opportunities available with each of the major forms of transportation. As for terminals, regardless of who owns or manages them, they all must maintain grounds and roads; do maintenance for which carpenters, electricians, plumbers, painters, and other craftsmen are required; provide security and clerical functions. There is also opportunity for unskilled laborers, typists, accountants, and computer specialists.

In large terminals there is a need for public relations staff, specialists in personnel, planners, and purchasing agents. The top positions would be those of manager and assistant manager, posts for which several years of experience are required.

Most terminals rent space to concessions: restaurants, newsstands, car rental agencies, gift shops, and in large city terminals, stores of all kinds. Working in a restaurant or store would provide temporary employment and give you an opportunity to check for other openings in the field you want to enter.

The VGM Career Horizons book, *Opportunities in Airline Careers,* contains a chapter on airports and it touches on job opportunities at airport terminals.

TRAVEL AGENCIES

Travel agents secure plane, train, or bus tickets as well as reservations for rental cars and hotel rooms for customers. However, such an agent would not handle the shipping of a horse or household goods. 19,000 travel agents in the country account for 65 percent of all airline tickets sold.

What makes the job of travel agent one of the most difficult in the transportation business is the never ending confusion surrounding airline schedules and fares. At one time it was said that an agent could compute as many as twenty different fares between Boston and Washington, depending on the carrier, type of service, time of day, day of the week, length of stay in Washington, type of equipment flown, and age of the passenger or relationship to the purchaser of the tickets.

To set up a client's long journey with numerous stop-overs may require calls to several carriers for the latest information on schedules and fares. Many travel agencies have computer terminals tied into an airline's reservations system which is a great help for obtaining information and confirming reservations on *that* carrier, but it calls for a real knowledge of the business nevertheless.

If you have patience, and can stand pressure, this could become an interesting career. Generally speaking, the pay is not what it might be considering the long hours and hard work, but there is one good fringe benefit, free "educational trips" which airlines and hotels offer, hoping you will refer business to them once you are familiar with their service.

Private employment agencies and your state employment security office are the best places to find out about possible openings in travel agencies as well as any large corporation which uses an employee rather than a travel agent to make all company travel arrangements. If you obtain no leads, contact the agencies yourself to see if any of them could use a beginner who is eager to learn the business. A high school diploma is a must for a travel agent, and general familiarity with airline, Amtrak, and bus routes is essential.

For further information write The American Society of Travel Agents, Inc., 711 Fifth Avenue, New York, NY 10017.

Army transportation engineers learn how to maintain their equipment. (Photo: U.S. Army.)

CHAPTER 13

CAREERS IN
GOVERNMENT SERVICE

Do you know who is the largest employer in the United States, if not the world? The answer is the federal government and then there are also the state, county, and municipal governments too, to say nothing of the many public authorities, some of which operate transportation systems. Altogether, the number of men and women working for government totals somewhere between 3.5 and 4 million. Of course transportation-related jobs are not numerous in the state, county, and municipal categories and therefore you will find your best opportunities probably exist in Uncle Sam's worldwide operations.

Even though the 1980s ushered in a cutback in government expenditures and reduction in the number of government employees, certain functions must continue. The military received additional billions while other government services were cut. The armed forces are the best place to start our survey of jobs because while we have a military establishment made up of volunteers the door is wide open to young men and women who can qualify for admission. What makes military service so attractive is the opportunity to obtain vocational training. At a time when education is expensive and beyond the reach of many, it makes sense to investigate a career with one of the services.

THE ARMED FORCES

The four principal military services, Air Force, Army, Marines (actually a branch of the Navy), and the Navy offer a wide range of career opportunities in clerical and administrative work, electrical and electronic occupations, and hundreds of other specialties, many of which are related to transportation.

Transportation is essential to all of the services. You may enlist in any one of a variety of programs which involve different combinations of active or reserve duty. Job training available to enlisted personnel may depend on the length of their service commitment, their general and technical aptitudes, personal preferences, and most of all, the needs of the service at that time.

Space limitations make it impossible to detail the career opportunities available in each of the services so we shall discuss the opportunities in the Marine Corps. In the courses selected for mention here we have included only those which train you in a skill which is transferable to civilian work should you decide not to remain in the service. The numeral following each of the courses indicates the number of weeks of training required. Remember that the courses included below are only a few of those actually offered.

Aircraft Maintenance: Aviation Maintenance Administration (7), Aviation Safety Equipment (9), Aviation Structure Mechanic (9), Aviation Hydraulic Mechanic (7), Basic Helicopter Course (6).

Air Traffic Control & Enlisted Flight Crews: Aerial Navigator (26), Airborne Radio Operator (16), Air Traffic Controller (8).

Avionics: Avionics Technician (12), Advanced First Term Avionics (26), Aviation Electrian Mate (11), Precision Measuring Equipment Technician (3), Avionics Technician Intermediate (28).

Electronics Maintenance: Aviation Radio Technician (9), Aviation Radio Repairer (20), Meteorological Equipment Maintenance (18), Aviation Radar Technician (17), Ground Radar Technician (27), Aviation Fire Control Technician (7).

Motor Transport: Fuels and Electrical Systems Repair (11), Basic Automotive Mechanic (12), Metal Body Repair (8), Advanced Automotive Mechanic (16).

Transportation: Defense Advanced Traffic Management (3), Installation Traffic Management (4).

There are many excellent benefits for those serving in the Armed Forces. In the Marine Corps, for example, you can earn 30 days vacation a year, obtain very inexpensive life insurance, low-cost dental and medical care, and you may visit the commissary and post exchange where you can do your shopping and find year-round bargain prices. Best of all, you can retire after twenty years of service with a generous pension. There is also a Marine Reserve Corps which enables you to receive the same vocational training and then return to civilian life, provided you spend one weekend a month at your Marine Reserve Unit, and two weeks each summer at a major military installation.

The other services have similar programs and if you request information about enlisting, you will be provided with full details of the latest program.

Don't ignore the army as a possible means of entering the transportation field. It operates its own airline, its own traffic control system, and of course motorized equipment of all kinds.

Each of the services publishes pamphlets which describe entrance requirements, training and advancement opportunities, and other aspects of military life. These publications are available at all recruiting stations, most state employment security offices, and in high schools, colleges, and public libraries. Consult your telephone book for the office of the nearest recruiting office which will be listed under United States Government, or write the following:

US Army Recruiting Command, Fort Sheridan, IL 60037.

USAF Recruiting Service, Directorate of Recruiting Operations, Randolph Air Force Base, TX 78148.

Director, Personnel Procurement Division, Headquarters, US Marine Corps, Washington, DC 20380.

Navy Opportunity Information Center, P.O. Box 2000, Pelham Manor, NY 10803.

Commandant (G-PMR), US Coast Guard, Washington, DC 20590.

THE NAVY MILITARY SEALIFT COMMAND

One unusual branch of the service is the Navy's Military Sealift Command which employs civilians both ashore and at sea.

MSC has a variety of positions on its ships such as those for licensed steam and diesel engineers; licensed deck officers; radio officers; deck and refrigeration engineers; able seamen; oilers and firemen-watertenders; electricians and machinists; yeoman-storekeepers; and cooks/bakers. Competition is keen for most positions; however, the greater the skill an applicant has, the better the chances for employment. On shore the MSC utilizes naval architects, marine engineers, marine transportation specialists, and computer specialists.

Applicants for positions at sea must have the appropriate US Coast Guard Merchant Marine documents or validated documents with the necessary endorsement. Apply at one of the following: Military Sealift Command, Atlantic, Civilian Personnel Office (L-22), Military Ocean Terminal, Bayonne, NJ 07002, or at the Naval Supply Center, Oakland, CA 94625.

THE PANAMA CANAL

Among the great peaceful endeavors of mankind which have contributed significantly to world progress, the construction of the Panama Canal stands as an awe-inspiring achievement. The enterprise was made possible by American ingenuity and ideals, without which, as President Theodore Roosevelt once said, "the Canal would not have been built."

The canal is 50 miles long from deep water in the Atlantic to deep water in the Pacific. It was cut through one of the narrowest places and at one of the lowest saddles of the Isthmus. A ship is raised or lowered 85 feet in three stages. It takes about nine hours to go through the canal.

In 1980 there were 8,626 employees of whom 1,027 were part-time or temporary and only 24 percent were United States citizens. Under the Panama Canal Treaty of 1977 citizens of Panama are given priority in employment. Recruitment is done in the United States for those jobs which cannot be filled in Panama. In 1982 only maritime specialists such as ship pilots and tugboat masters, plus a few highly skilled craft personnel were recruited outside of the Isthmus.

In view of the limited employment prospects and the fact that on December 31, 1999, the United States will transfer the entire Canal to the Republic of Panama, it would hardly seem worth mentioning the canal. However, since it is a vital waterway, some readers might consider it a likely employer. It is, but in a limited sense.

If after reading this you feel that you might qualify for a position with the Commission or want to inquire about employment possibilities, write the Panama Canal Commission, 425-13th Street, NW, Washington, DC 20004.

UNITED STATES CUSTOMS SERVICE

The Customs Service was one of the first government agencies created in 1789, its purpose being to assess and collect the revenue on imported merchandise and to enforce customs and related laws. Today it has some 14,000 employees, most of whom are located at the nearly 300 ports of entry. A few are assigned to overseas posts.

The Customs Service enforces its own as well as approximately 400 laws and regulations for 40 other federal agencies. It also conducts a variety of anti-smuggling programs.

To get some idea of the size of the job which faces the Customs Service, consider that in 1980 more than 297 million people entered the United States and passed through customs. In addition, imports were processed valued at over $238 billion. They required more than 4.3 million formal entries (for those over $250 in value), a staggering amount of paper work. The service collected more than $8.23 billion in duties and taxes, and seized over $3.5 billion worth of illegal narcotics and dangerous drugs.

All of this spells a challenge of a unique sort and although this work has nothing to do with the actual transporting of people or goods, it is, nevertheless, an essential part of our transportation system in that travel and shipping of goods to the United States are involved.

Here are brief descriptions of the principal career positions with the service.

Customs Inspectors are probably the only customs employees with whom the public is familiar. At airports and other ports of entry they inspect your baggage to ensure compliance with the tariff laws and try to detect smugglers.

Inspectors review ship and plane manifests as they examine cargo and control shipments which are transferred under bond to ports throughout the United States. Customs inspectors are the nation's front line defenders against smuggling as they work in cooperation with customs special agents, patrol officers, and import specialists, as well as the FBI and the Drug Enforcement Administration. As part of the law enforcement team, inspectors perform personal searches, seize contraband, and apprehend violators. They may also be required to wear side arms.

Special Agents comprise a highly trained investigative force of the service whose purpose is to frustrate the efforts of smugglers. Aided by complex radio communications networks which provide critical data on the activities of suspects, they follow the journey of contraband from its entry along our borders and coastlines. Special Agents are assigned to duty stations in most ports of entry and may be called on to travel during the course of their work.

Customs Patrol Officers carry out the difficult task of detecting and apprehending violators of the 400 statutes enforced by the service. They prevent smuggling into the country and may serve anywhere in the United States from along the frozen northern border to the deserts of the southwest, from urban waterfronts to secluded coastlines. No two assignments are alike, nor are two working days.

Import Specialists assess the rate of duties, an activity which makes the service a major revenue producing agency of the government. They examine import entry documents, check to see that the imported merchandise agrees with the description, then classify the merchandise under the tariff schedules to determine the correct duty required. Import Specialists become experts in one or more lines of merchandise and in order to make sure that their expertise remains up to date, they often examine selected shipments.

Customs Aids perform semitechnical duties which require a specialized knowledge of provisions of customs laws and regulations. They assist inspectors and other specialists in the service.

There are other interesting career possibilities too.

Canine Enforcement Officers train and use dogs to enforce customs laws pertaining to the smuggling of marijuana, narcotics, and dangerous drugs.

A *Customs Pilot* is part of a program of air surveillance of illegal traffic crossing United States borders by air, land, or sea. Pilots also apprehend, arrest, and search violators of customs and related laws.

Customs Chemists play an important part in protecting the nation's health and safety as well as the security of the country's commerce. They are called upon to analyze imported merchandise ranging from textile fibers to contraband narcotics.

In addition to the above specialist positions there are numerous data processing positions in the Washington headquarters, to say nothing of the usual clerical openings.

Customs jobs are filled and administered under the competitive civil service system. Since the educational and experience requirements for each of the jobs vary, it is best to check with the nearest Federal Job Information Center or the Customs Service itself to learn about openings and what the requirements are for each.

For further information write the United States Customs Service, Headquarters Personnel Branch, 1301 Constitution Avenue, NW, Washington, DC 20229.

AIR TRAFFIC CONTROL

On August 3, 1980, federal air traffic controllers began a nationwide strike which was declared illegal. Their union had rejected a final offer for a new contract but in spite of the walkout about 60 percent of the 14,200 scheduled daily airline flights continued to operate. Supervisors and non-strikers manned the radar-operated control towers.

President Reagan warned the strikers that unless they returned to work by 11:00 A.M. on August 5, they would be immediately fired. After most of the 13,000 controllers refused to report to their towers, the Federal Aviation Administration sent out the first of the dismissal notices. Although controllers in some other countries refused to clear departures of flights to the United States, this action fizzled as President Reagan remained adamant in his stand against the strikers. Military controllers and supervisors continued to handle the towers with those controllers who had not gone out on strike. All airline flight schedules were cut back and a long-range program was instituted for hiring and training controllers. In 1982 the union announced plans to disband.

Although controllers have been badly needed, the Federal Aviation Administration, which is in charge of all air traffic control activities, has not let down its standards. Here is how the administration defines the required background:

"General Experience: Progressively responsible experience in administrative, technical, or other work which demonstrated potential for learning and performing air traffic control work.

"Specialized Experience: Experience in a military or civilian air traffic facility which demonstrated possession of the knowledge, skills, and abilities required to perform the level of work of the specialization for which application is made."

It may be possible to substitute certain education and flight training for experience. But you must check with the Federal Aviation Administration regarding current qualifications. In any case, you must pass a physical examination including tests for color vision, and also a comprehensive written test and be interviewed. The maximum age of thirty was established for entry into a tower but this requirement may be changed.

Controllers normally work a forty-hour week in FAA control towers at airports using radio, radar, electronic computers, telephones, traffic control lights, and other devices for communication.

Controllers give taxiing instructions to aircraft on the ground, takeoff instructions and clearances to incoming planes. At busy locations these duties are rotated among staff members about every two hours. A controller must work quickly, and demands increase as the traffic mounts, especially when there are poor flying conditions and traffic stacks up. Brief rest periods provide some relief but they are not always possible. Shift work is necessary in this occupation.

Before the controllers' strike the FAA employed over eleven thousand controllers at more than four hundred airports. A few towers are located outside the continental United States in Alaska, Hawaii, Puerto Rico, the Virgin Islands, and American Samoa.

Promotion from trainee to a higher grade professional controller depends on satisfactory progression in his or her training program. Trainees who do not successfully complete the training courses are terminated or reassigned from their controller positions.

During the first year a trainee is on probation but afterwards may advance from positions backing up professional controllers to primary positions of responsibility. It takes a controller from three to six years of experience to reach peak performance.

Some professional controllers are selected for research activities with FAA's National Aviation Facilities Experimental Center in Atlantic City, New Jersey. Others may serve as instructors. Trainees receive from fifteen to nineteen weeks of instruction at the FAA Academy in Oklahoma City, Oklahoma, and then are assigned to a tower for on-the-job training under close supervision.

Additional information about Air Traffic Control is contained in the VGM Career Horizons *Opportunities in Airline Careers.* For further information about employment opportunities, consult the Civil Service Commission, 1900 E Street, NW, Washington, DC 20006.

FEDERAL REGULATORY AGENCIES

Recently there has been a trend in the federal government to deregulate. The Civil Aeronautics Board, for example, is supposed to be mostly disbanded by 1984.

It should be noted that many of the positions in the federal agencies concerned with transportation call for specialists in the fields of accounting, data processing, engineering, finance, highway traffic, personnel, planning, research, safety, and transportation. In addition there are the usual office support positions in the clerical areas.

For information about current job openings contact your nearest state employment security office or the United States Civil Service Commission (see above for address).

Department of Transportation

This agency establishes the nation's transportation policy. Under its umbrella there are eight administrations. Their jurisdictions include highway planning, development and construction; urban mass transit; railroads; aviation; and the safety of waterways, ports, highways, and oil and gas pipelines. Decisions made by this department in conjunction with the appropriate state and local officials strongly affect other programs such as land planning, energy conservation, scarce resource utilization, and technological change.

One of the agencies which is under the Department of Transportation is the United States Coast Guard. It maintains a system of rescue vessels, aircraft, and communications facilities to carry out its function of saving life and property in the high seas and navigable waters of the United States.

For further information about the Department of Transportation contact the Office of Public Affairs (DOT) Information Center, 400 Seventh Street SW, Washington, DC 20590.

Federal Maritime Commission

This commission regulates the waterborne foreign and domestic offshore commerce of the country. It assures that United States international trade is open to all nations on fair and equitable terms, and protects against unauthorized activity in the water-borne commerce of the United States.

For further information contact the Office of the Chairman, Federal Maritime Commission, 1100 L Street NW, Washington, DC 20573.

Interstate Commerce Commission

This commission, popularly known as the ICC, is responsible for regulating interstate surface transportation including trains, trucks, buses, inland waterways and coastal shipping, and freight handlers. The regulatory laws vary depending on the type of transportation, but they generally involve certification of carriers seeking to provide transportation for the public rates, adequacy of service, purchases, and mergers. The ICC is responsible for assuring that the carriers it regulates will provide the public with rates and services that are fair and reasonable.

For further information contact the Office of Communications, Interstate Commerce Commission, Washington, DC 20423.

National Transportation Safety Board

This agency seeks to assure that all types of transportation in the United States are conducted safely. The Board investigates accidents, conducts studies, and makes recommendations to government agencies. It also regulates the procedures for reporting accidents and promotes the safe transport of hazardous materials by government and private industry.

For further information contact the Office of Government and Public Affairs, National Transportation Safety Board, 800 Independence Avenue SW, Washington, DC 20594.

STATE AND LOCAL REGULATORY AGENCIES

Another layer of agencies regulating intrastate transportation will be found in each of the states. They have various names, the most usual being the Public Utilities Commission although you may find Department of Transportation or even Railroad Commission. Since their jurisdictions are limited to operations within the state, most of them offer limited career opportunities. You can obtain the name and address of your state agency from your public library or by writing to the Secretary of State at your state capital. You may find openings for drivers and mechanics with your state highway department. Contact your nearest state employment security office or the state civil service commission for information about current job openings.

In some of the larger municipalities you may find agencies which regulate taxi and limousine service within the city borders, or the operation of the transit system. There may be an agency which

Naval training includes extensive practice with large and small aircraft, above. Customs Patrol Officers check carefully for hidden cargo, below. (Photos: U.S. Navy Great Lakes Training Station and U.S. Customs.)

provides automobiles and drivers to transport municipal employees on official business. As in the case of the state, the highway department may offer job opportunities for drivers, mechanics, and other job assignments. Consult your telephone book under the listing for your city for the proper name of such agencies or visit the civil service commission.

Overleaf: The professional airline pilot is the leader of a highly trained flight crew. (Photo: Delta Air Lines.)

CHAPTER 14

YOUR CAREER IN TRANSPORTATION

By now you have seen that transportation, like other industries, offers both advantages and disadvantages. It might be helpful to enumerate them.

ADVANTAGES

Since transportation is as essential to the nation as agriculture you will experience a higher degree of job security working in it than in many other businesses. Unlike some industries which may lay off many employees or close down altogether during economic recessions, a carrier may be forced to retrench somewhat, but not to the extent that many harder-hit firms might.

If you like to travel, you may find a position which will enable you to do so. Even though you hold a desk job in an airline, bus, or rail company, you may enjoy free travel privileges along with other fringe benefits. Best of all, this business has glamour because travel can be stimulating and fun.

DISADVANTAGES

On the other hand, transportation is a seven-day-a-week, around-the-clock business. This means you may be assigned to work the graveyard shift (4:00 P.M. to midnight) or the night shift (midnight to 8:00 A.M.), to say nothing of Saturdays, Sundays, and holidays. Furthermore, if your job involves working on buses, planes, trains, ships, trucks, or other vehicles which travel long distances, you may be away from home a lot. Because air, marine, and ground transport runs year-round in every kind of weather, you can anticipate encountering all types of weather conditions and occasionally dangerous travel conditions.

YOUR NEXT STEP

After finishing this book, if you think a career in transportation is for you, learn all you can about that branch of the industry and the jobs which interest you. Find out what education or specialized training is required, so that you can start preparing yourself as soon as possible. Discuss your ideas with other people whose judgment you respect, or preferably, someone in the industry.

To summarize what has been said before, transportation jobs require one of four levels of educational training:

1. High school for unskilled entry positions such as cleaners, custodians, food handlers, mail room clerks, and drivers.

2. Technical or vocational school for mechanics, secretaries, bookkeepers, pilots, and seamen.

3. An undergraduate degree for many entry positions in supervisory or professional positions.

4. Graduate degree principally for professionals such as engineers, lawyers, librarians, computer specialists, management specialists, and public relations practitioners.

Regardless of the educational requirements of the job you are contemplating, start today to chart your future so that you can make it happen. Lack of money need not discourage you or keep you from pursuing a career which calls for technical or college training. It is quite possible you can obtain a scholarship, loan or grant, earn some of the money while you are studying, or find other types of financial assistance.

FINDING A JOB

When you are ready to start your job search consider the following suggestions:

Read one or two books on how to find a job. Ask your school or public librarian for recommendations and check the Suggested Reading in the appendices of this book.

If you are still in school or college, ask the guidance counselor or someone in the college personnel office for job leads and advice.

Tell everyone you know about your job hunting goal because they may hear of openings.

Register at your state employment security office and at private employment agencies. (See the listing of state offices in the white pages of your telephone directory for the nearest employment security office, and in the yellow pages turn to the heading: Employment Agencies.)

Study the help wanted advertisements in your local newspapers.

Visit the offices of transport operators where you hope to find work and ask if you may file an application. Write to the out-of-town companies.

Finally, don't become discouraged. Keep up your search every day. Remember that you *will* find a job if you look hard enough.

THE FUTURE IS YOURS

Few industries offer the variety of job opportunities that transportation does. Most importantly transportation is a business which places an awesome responsibility on you. For example, a nut which is not properly tightened, an underinflated tire, or a restraining block of wood not removed from a wing joint could be the cause of tragedy. During the years ahead, the lives of many men, women, and children could depend on how carefully and conscientiously you perform your duties. As you can see, this is a career not to be undertaken lightly.

PRINCIPAL TRANSPORTATION LABOR UNIONS

Air Line Employees Association, International
5600 South Central Avenue
Chicago, IL 60638

Air Line Pilots Association
1625 Massachusetts Avenue, NW
Washington, DC 20036

Allied Pilots Association
P.O. Box 5524
Arlington, TX 76011

Aircraft Mechanics Fraternal Association
4150 Cypress Road
St. Ann, MO 63074

Amalgamated Transit Union
5025 Wisconsin Avenue, NW
Washington, DC 20016

American Train Dispatchers Association
1401 South Harlem Avenue
Berwyn, IL 60402

Association of Flight Attendants
1625 Massachusetts Avenue, NW
Washington, DC 20036

Association of Flight Engineers
1625 Massachusetts Avenue, NW
Washington, DC 20036

Association of Professional Flight Attendants
1220 North State Street
Chicago, IL 60610

Brotherhood of Locomotive Engineers
1365 Ontario Street
Cleveland, OH 44114

Brotherhood of Maintenance of Way Employees
12050 Woodward Avenue
Detroit, MI 48203

Brotherhood of Marine Officers
95 River Street
Hoboken, NJ 07030

Brotherhood of Railroad Signalmen
601 West Golf Road
Mt. Prospect, IL 60056

Brotherhood of Railway, Airline and Steamship Clerks,
    Freight Handlers, Express and Station Employees
3 Research Place
Rockville, MD 20850

Brotherhood of the Railway Carmen of the United States and
    Canada
4929 Main Street
Kansas City, MO 64112

International Brotherhood of Teamsters
25 Louisiana Avenue, NW
Washington, DC 20001

International Longshoremen's and Warehousemen's Union
1188 Franklin
San Francisco, CA 94109

International Longshoremen's Association
17 Battery Place
New York, NY 10004

International Organization of Masters, Mates and Pilots
39 Broadway
New York, NY 10006

Marine Firemen's Union (Pacific Coast Marine Firemen,
    Oilers, Watertenders and Wipers Association)
240 Second Street
San Francisco, CA 94105

National Association of Air Traffic Specialists
Wheaton Plaza North
Wheaton, MD 20902

National Marine Engineers Beneficial Association
444 North Capitol
Washington, DC 20001

National Maritime Union
346 17th Street
New York, NY 10011

Railroad Yardmasters of America
1411 Peterson Avenue
Park Ridge, IL 60068

Seafarers International Union
675 Fourth Avenue
Brooklyn, NY 11232

Transport Workers Union of America
1980 Broadway
New York, NY 10014

United Transportation Union
14600 Detroit Avenue
Cleveland, OH 44107

APPENDIX B

BIBLIOGRAPHY OF RELATED READING

The following books should prove interesting and helpful to the man or woman who wants further information about transportation careers. You may find additional current information about transportation in magazines and journals. It is suggested that you consult the *Reader's Guide to Periodical Literature and* the *Business Periodicals Index* which list all articles that have appeared in several dozen leading magazines. These indexes are easy to use and can be found in many public libraries.

Arco Editorial Board, *Bus Maintainer—Bus Mechanic.* New York: Arco Publishing Inc., 1972.

‗‗‗‗ *Bus Operator; Conductor.* New York: Arco Publishing Inc., 1970.

‗‗‗‗ *Surface Line Dispatcher.* New York: Arco Publishing Inc., 1974.

Asa, Donald S., *Introduction to Trucking.* Phoenix, Ariz: D & A Publishing Co., 1978.

Bolles, Richard N., *What Color Is Your Parachute? A practical manual for job hunters and career changers.* Berkeley, Calif.: Ten Speed Press, 1981.

Boulton, W. H., *Pageant of Transport Through the Ages.* New York: Arno Press, 1977.

Cadin, Martin, *Boeing 707.* New York: Ballantine Books, 1959. (Paperback)

Catalyst, Inc., *What To Do With the Rest of Your Life: the Catalyst career guide for women in the 80's.* New York: Simon & Schuster, 1980.

Drury, Jolyon, *Airports.* New York: Nichols Publishing Company, 1978.

Figler, Howard, *The Complete Job-Search Handbook: all the skills you need to get any job and have a good time doing it.* New York: Holt Rinehart & Winston, 1979.

Garrison, Paul, *How the Air Traffic Control System Works*. Blue Ridge Summit, Pa.: TAB Books, 1979.

Goodfellow, Thomas M., *Your Future in Railroading*. New York: Richards Rosen Press, Inc., 1976.

Jawin, Ann Juliano, *A Woman's Guide to Career Preparation: Scholarships, Grants, and Loans*. Garden City, N.Y.: Anchor Books, 1979.

McLintock, Gordon E., *Your Future in the Merchant Marine*. New York: Richards Rosen Press, Inc., 1978.

Morton, Alexander C., *The Official 1980-81 Guide to Travel Agents and Travel Careers:* Travel Press, 1981.

Paradis, Adrian A., *Two Hundred Million Miles a Day*. Philadelphia: Chilton Book Co., 1969.

Randall, Lyman, *Your Future as an Airlines Stewardess-Steward*. New York: Richards Rosen Press, Inc., 1978.

Rich, Elizabeth, *What It's Like To be a Flight Attendant*. Briarcliff Manor, N.Y.: Stein and Day, 1981.

Richardson, J. D., *Essentials of Aviation Management*. Dubuque, Ia.: Kendall/Hunt, 1977.

Sabin, Arthur J., *You Can Learn To Fly*. Mountain View, Calif.: Anderson World, Inc., 1979.

Serling, Robert J., *The Only Way To Fly*. Garden City, N.Y.: Doubleday, 1976.

Shanahan, William F., *College— Yes or No*. New York: Arco Publishing Inc., 1980.

Smith, Peter, *AirFreight*. Salem, N.H.: Faber and Faber, 1974.

Stilley, Frank, *Here Is Your Career: Airline Pilot*. New York: G. P. Putnam's Sons, 1978.

Taneja, Nawal K., *Airlines in Transition*. Lexington, Mass.: Lexington Books, 1981.

——— *Commercial Airlines Industry: Managerial Practices and Policies*. Lexington, Mass.: Lexington Books, 1976.

Wyckoff, Daryl, and Maister, David H., *The Domestic Airline Industry*. Lexington, Mass.: Lexington Books, 1977.